I can confidently say I've never read .... easier than *A Mother's Guide to Raising Herself.* No matter how long you've resided in "should land," stifled your voice, or abandoned your dreams, this compassionate guide offers real hope. Through unifying humor, relatable examples, and heartfelt honesty, Sarah Bragg shows us how to honor ourselves as we raise our kids. Let *A Mother's Guide* bring peace to your soul and more YOU to the brave story of your life.

Rachel Macy Stafford, *New York Times* bestselling author, speaker, and special education teacher

Sarah Bragg has cornered the market on heartfully and honestly rendering what modern motherhood looks like. She writes with an elegant compassion and understanding about what it means for parents caught in the modern tension of raising themselves while also raising kids.

Knox McCoy, cohost of *The Popcast* and author of *All Things Reconsidered*

Sarah Bragg gives women blankets of grace in *A Mother's Guide to Raising Herself.* Her stories are relatable and funny, and I found myself nodding my head throughout every chapter. I wish I had read something like this earlier in my own motherhood journey. It would have made those long days just a little bit sweeter to know I wasn't alone.

Laura Tremaine, author of *Share Your Stuff. I'll Go First.*

Sarah Bragg shows up like a friend in the thick of our hardest days, and we find ourselves breathing again. Gentle, funny, and unflinchingly honest, this book is a bouquet of vital truths and timely reminders.

Shannan Martin, author of *The Ministry of Ordinary Places* and *Falling Free*

This must-read book is not only refreshingly honest but incredibly transformational in redefining what we think we're "supposed to be" as moms versus what matters most. Sarah's heart shines brightly in ways that embolden all mothers to be brave enough to look in the mirror, focus on our inner beauty, and gain the freedom to unapologetically live out loud and become the mothers we were born to be.

Deborah L. Tillman, global parenting and childcare specialist and Lifetime Television's *America's Supernanny*

With honest, heart-on-sleeve storytelling, Sarah brings a refreshing view of motherhood that our culture desperately needs right now. In a world constantly pushing us to "thrive" in all circumstances, she invites us into a shame-free narrative where showing up and being present are the keys to cultivating meaningful relationships with ourselves and our children. Sarah is a truth-teller, a guide, and an instant friend. Her words are a much-needed balm for the weary and for those of us who simply need a reminder to be courageous in scripting a braver story.

Hannah Brencher, author of *Fighting Forward* and *Come Matter Here*

I have had some of my most defining conversations as a mom sitting across the table from Sarah Bragg. Her courageous honesty about what it means to be a mother as well as a growing, learning, thriving human is everything. I have a feeling I will be gifting this book to moms for years to come.

Kristen Ivy, president of Orange and Parent Cue

A MOTHER'S GUIDE TO

RAISING HERSELF

WHAT PARENTING TAUGHT ME
ABOUT LIFE, FAITH, AND MYSELF

SARAH BRAGG

ZONDERVAN
BOOKS

ZONDERVAN BOOKS

A Mother's Guide to Raising Herself
Copyright © 2021 by Sarah Bragg

Requests for information should be addressed to:
Zondervan, *3900 Sparks Dr. SE, Grand Rapids, Michigan 49546*

Zondervan titles may be purchased in bulk for educational, business, fundraising, or sales promotional use. For information, please email SpecialMarkets@Zondervan.com.

ISBN 978-0-310-36136-7 (audio)

Library of Congress Cataloging-in-Publication Data

Names: Bragg, Sarah, 1978- author.
Title: A mother's guide to raising herself : what parenting taught me about life, faith, and myself / Sarah Bragg.
Description: Grand Rapids : Zondervan, 2021. | Includes bibliographical references. | Summary: "Raising great kids starts with raising yourself well, yet it's all too easy to lose our identity in the daily struggle of motherhood. Popular podcaster and mom Sarah Bragg offers refreshing wisdom and shame-free practical help to becoming your best and truest self in A Mother's Guide to Raising Herself"-- Provided by publisher.
Identifiers: LCCN 2021001616 (print) | LCCN 2021001617 (ebook) | ISBN 9780310361343 (trade paperback) | ISBN 9780310361350 (ebook)
Subjects: LCSH: Motherhood--Religious aspects--Christianity. | Self-awareness (Sensitivity) | Mothers--Religious life. | BISAC: RELIGION / Christian Living / Women's Interests | RELIGION / Christian Living / Parenting
Classification: LCC BV4529.18 .B725 2021 (print) | LCC BV4529.18 (ebook) | DDC 248.8/431--dc23
LC record available at https://lccn.loc.gov/2021001616
LC ebook record available at https://lccn.loc.gov/2021001617

All Scripture quotations are taken from the Holy Bible, New Living Translation. © 1996, 2004, 2015 by Tyndale House Foundation. Used by permission of Tyndale House Publishers, Inc., Carol Stream, Illinois 60188. All rights reserved.

Published in association with Yates & Yates, www.yates2.com.

Art direction: Curt Diepenhorst
Cover design: Connie Gabbert
Cover images: Africa Studio / Magenta 10 / Shutterstock
Interior design: Sara Colley

Printed in the United States of America

21 22 23 24 25 26 27 28 29 /LSC/ 13 12 11 10 9 8 7 6 5 4 3 2 1

To my daughters, Sinclair and Rory. This book is for you and because of you.

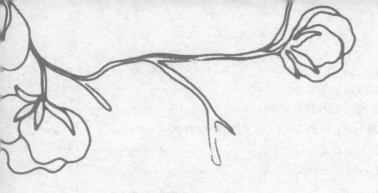

CONTENTS

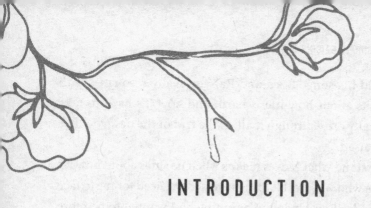

INTRODUCTION

BORN AND RAISED

I thought having kids was all about *them* being born and raised. What I didn't know was how much *they* were going to raise *me*. On May 31, 2008, when Sinclair Bragg was born, I, too, was born. I just didn't know it yet.

She learned to walk. So did I—I learned to walk into who I *really* am.

She learned to talk. So did I—I learned to speak differently to myself.

She learned to face her fear of the dark. So did I—I learned to face the fear of failure.

So much of who I am today is because of Sinclair and Rory, the girls I birthed. But it hasn't been easy. Raising kids is the hardest thing I've ever done. I've never wanted to quit something more in my life. This doesn't mean I don't love them. It just means raising kids is hard—harder than I'd ever imagined.

Not long ago, I was listening to one of my favorite John Mayer albums, and his song "Born and Raised" really resonated with me. He talks about how life is hard, and how it's hard to fake who you really are. Through it all, at the end of the day, you'll be born and raised.

I understand what Mayer means when he sings about how it's hard to fake who you are. Nothing revealed the need for me to face who I was, who I pretended to be, and who I wanted to be more than having kids. Raising kids has been the greatest catalyst for growth in me. I am a different person now than before I became a mother. It wasn't a painless change, but while I don't like going through hard things, I wouldn't change who I've become.

Raising myself has taken time. It's taken hardship. It's taken wrestling with the vulnerability and uncertainty of it all. But it's worth it. And for that reason, I am forever grateful to the two girls who have helped raise me.

Maybe you also feel like you have been born and raised in a way you weren't expecting. Maybe you feel like me—born into something uncertain, unknown, and sometimes unpleasant. Being born into something often feels unpleasant. As beautiful as a physical birth is, it's generally painful and even scary (for both mother and child).

When Sinclair was born, I remember reading all. the. books. I wanted to know *everything*. I wanted to know all there was to know about birth plans, schedules, nursing, milestones, and baby food. Knowledge was like a security blanket that would keep me safe as I walked into this unknown territory. I had always been a good student who believed I could accomplish anything I set my mind to. I thought if I studied child-rearing the way I'd studied the piano, I would be just fine. I know—famous last words, right?

Well, even though I acquired the knowledge, it still turned

out to be far harder than I'd imagined. I still felt lost. It also revealed something surprising about me—I wasn't a natural at this mothering thing. I still had a lot to learn, most of which couldn't be found in a book. Much of what I needed to learn was going to come through showing up, through being born into this uncertain and unfamiliar place and allowing these circumstances and people to raise me to be who I am supposed to be.

But hear me on this: I fought the growing-up process. I didn't start working on raising myself until Sinclair was nearly five and my second daughter, Rory, was a preschooler. Until that point, I still believed if I just read more or prayed for my kids to change, things would be better. I prayed and prayed, but my kids didn't change. They still pushed all my buttons. They still made messes everywhere. And I still felt unhappy and discontented.

I wish I could say there was a catalyst, a turning point, that incited the change in me. But I can't pinpoint one. Instead, I think I began to change *when I started being honest with myself.* I started journaling again, something I hadn't done since I was a young girl. (Someone will likely need to burn these journals when I die.) I started processing my thoughts and feelings in a very honest way. I started working on who I was. I started seeing that the things I wanted for my daughters were the same things I wanted for myself.

I wanted them to be free to be who they are. *Me too.*

I wanted them to feel loved no matter what. *Me too.*

I wanted them to feel accepted. *Me too.*

I wanted them to know they are enough exactly as they are. *Me too.*

I wanted them to know they are strong and brave. *Me too.*

The question was, how could I instill these truths in my girls if I didn't believe them for myself? I needed to experience a sort of rebirth. Not the kind I was taught about in Sunday school, but the kind that required me to embody the lessons I had heard all my life, the kind that required me to live into those lessons as a mother. If I wanted my girls to believe all of these big ideas, I needed to become the sort of woman who lived out of my own belief in them.

I had to acknowledge my inclinations toward perfectionism, fear, shame, and inauthenticity. I had to confront some hard things about myself and be willing to push through them. Raising myself was going to require change. I would need to be brave enough to dare to imagine a different story.

Rachel Macy Stafford writes in her book *Live Love Now*, "Perfect parenting is not required to raise resilient, compassionate, and capable adults. Better off are the kids whose parents are willing to rewrite their job description and admit they are up for the task of learning, discovering, and growing right alongside their children."[1] That's exactly what this book is about. It's about rewriting the story. It's about sharing what I've learned through parenting that has in turn raised me. Parenting forced me to take a hard look at what I believed about my life, my faith, and myself to see what is true. If something is true for my daughters, then it is true for me.

I grew up in the South, in a very stereotypical American Christian faith where you went to church whenever the doors were open. I honestly loved it. I loved it because it was just a part of our life. It felt like a nice little bubble. However, as I've grown older, I realized that I didn't step out of that bubble until much later in life. It was a comfortable feeling, like I knew all the answers to all the questions. But I realized that remaining in that bubble, while it appeared to be safe, actually delayed a process of discovering and accepting myself. So many people go away to college or enter the workforce in their twenties and are given the opportunity to question what they believe about their life, their faith, and themselves. But I went to a Christian college and then became a professional Christian by working in and for churches. Raising kids was the catalyst that pushed me to really discover what I believe, and to believe it not just because a pastor told me to or because I read it in the Bible. In no way is my evolution a negative reflection on my parents. I think we can all look back at the way we were raised with both positivity and negativity. I fully expect my girls to do the same. Much of growing up, of raising ourselves, requires us to inspect where we came from, how it shaped us, and how it stands up to what we now know to be true.

In the pages that follow, I'm going to share different phrases I've learned over the years of parenting that have helped me grow up. Many of these phrases are ones I started teaching Sinclair and Rory, but ultimately I discovered I was teaching them to myself as well. I've raised myself on these phrases. I hope they can help you grow into yourself.

So here's my story. I hope it helps you realize you're not alone. I hope it has a ripple effect, making you brave enough to share *your* story. Because when we share our stories, we make the world around us a little better.

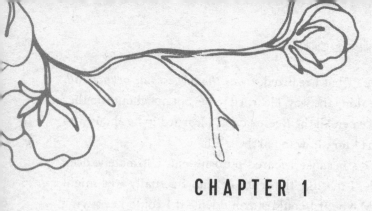

CHAPTER 1

TELL THE TRUTH

How many times have you said, "Tell the truth," to your kids? If you're anything like me, probably too many times to count.

"Did you get into Mom's makeup? Tell the truth."

"How many Reese's cups did you eat? Tell the truth."

"Did you finish your homework? Tell the truth."

"Did you throw a shoe at your sister? Tell the truth."

Apparently, we have a bunch of filthy liars in our house (resident author included).

When I became a mom, it felt like someone gave me a scepter and a sword, and I was supposed to reign over my subordinates, to keep them in order. I felt like I was supposed to get the truth out of them because, if I didn't, they would grow up to be big, fat liars. So I watched them like a hawk. I was smart and sharp. They couldn't get anything past me.

Can I be honest with you? Parenting like this was exhausting.

But here's what I realized: *I was the biggest liar of them all.* Somewhere along the way, I learned to lie, but not about whether or not I had eaten all the Reese's cups. I learned to lie about who I am. I didn't know how to tell the truth.

Maybe it's because I feared punishment. Ultimately, deep down inside, I felt like the truth of who I actually was might be wrong. Maybe if I could stay hidden—if I could keep lying in order to be accepted and keep the peace—I wouldn't get into trouble. I would be able to please everyone, and everyone would be happy.

Why did I think the truth was punishable?

When my girls were younger, I punished everything. I punished lies, and I punished the truth. If they lied, they were punished. If their truth was not my truth, they were punished. But what if, by punishing them this way, I was training them to lie? This concerned me, because I want them to be women who tell the truth about who they are without fear of judgment.

I recently heard Brené Brown talk with David Kessler on a podcast interview wherein he said, "Judgment requires punishment."[1] If I wanted my girls to grow up able to tell the truth about who they are, maybe I needed to change something in my parenting. So I started saying, "If you tell me the truth, you won't be punished." I wanted them to start practicing being able to tell whatever truth lives inside them. One of the greatest things we can do for ourselves (and our kids) is to start saying what is true on the inside and start making it true on the outside. Because often, what we say or do on the outside doesn't match what is true on the inside. And that incongruency is exhausting and phony.

I had to apply the same instruction to myself. I told myself

I wouldn't be punished for telling the truth. I started wrestling with who I am. I thought about it constantly. *Who am I, really?* I've spent my life being whoever other people want me to be. I've tried on personas like they were various styles of jeans, sucking in my stomach and pulling up the jeans by jumping up and down. Then, once they were finally zipped, I performed squats to stretch them a bit to see if they would fit.

Something that helped me begin to tell the truth about myself was the Enneagram, one of the most popular things to hit Christian culture since WWJD bracelets. In case you haven't heard, the Enneagram is a personality typing system that helps you understand who you are and how you relate to the world. I'm a type 3, which is the "achiever" or "performer." This definition nails me exactly. One of the notable characteristics of a 3 is the ability to read a room and figure out who you need to be to fit in. In many cases, this is a superpower that serves me well, but like all superpowers, it can also be my greatest weakness, my kryptonite. I used my superpower so often that I forgot to pay attention to who I *really* am.

Once I realized this, I started paying attention to who I became around other people. I paid attention to whether I was being real or performing. I paid attention to the truth that was deep inside.

What truth do you hold deep down inside, the truth you always feel like you have to lie about on the outside? Say it out loud, or write it in the margins of this book or in a journal. Just get it out. *Tell the truth.*

But start small. Because in order to eventually tackle the big things—like personality weaknesses and parenting issues—we need to build up the muscle of vulnerability. Starting small helps us do that. Maybe if we start by admitting who we are in the small things, we will be free to admit who we really are in the big things.

I'll go first.

Breakfast is overrated.
I will choose Starbucks over my local coffee shop
    every time.
School functions make me tired.
I don't like to volunteer at my daughters' school.
I hate costume parties.
I prefer eggs over easy on toast to scrambled.
I cuss (sometimes in front of my kids).
I don't know how to handle everything.
I need more than seven hours of sleep.
I like sleeping in on the weekends.

These are small things, but admitting them helps me think about bigger things. Another area in which I needed to be more myself was my weekly podcast, *Surviving Sarah*. It was easy for me to look around at other successful podcasts and try to mimic what they did. But I was ready to be more myself with the podcast, too. After journaling about who I am, what kinds of conversations I enjoy having, and what kinds of conversations make me uncomfortable, I started to draw boundaries around guests. I stopped saying yes to people I didn't want to have on the show, even if they were guests on other shows. Even if they were popular. I started saying yes to the guests *I* wanted to host, even though I knew I might lose listeners. I started to let the show reflect who I am instead of who I thought I was supposed to be.

The more I admitted these things to myself, the more I found and accepted who I am.

The more I accepted who I am, the more I needed to start voicing who I am out loud. I started being more honest with the person closest to me. I'm thankful to be married to a man who loves to talk as much as I do. We spend a lot of time talking once the girls go to bed. I'm thankful that in the last few years, we've been able to have some very honest conversations about our deepest vulnerabilities in parenting, life, and faith.

Part of figuring out who I am involved wrestling with the honest, vulnerable, sometimes scary thoughts and emotions in my heart and head, giving myself permission to feel and then vocalize them. I was waiting for the moment when I became Supermom; when, all of a sudden, I wanted to attend every school function or not go back to work or spend every Saturday morning snuggling in bed with my kids. This was the mom I thought I was supposed to be—a mom who loved every moment of motherhood. But when I finally acknowledged that wasn't who I am, or who I want to be, freedom followed.

Telling the truth about yourself will require a level of bravery. It might feel scary to show up as yourself. It might feel scary to do what you know, deep down, you should do. It might feel scary to say no when others say yes, or to say yes when others say no. That's why it will require bravery. It takes courage to be true to *yourself.*

It's risky to be the real you, to show up as your true self, to go against the crowd, to be different from your best friend or your family. But I want that for my girls. I want them to be brave enough to be their true selves.

The more I learned to tell the truth about myself, the more

I wanted my girls to tell the truth about themselves. If you have raised a strong-willed, highly emotional kid, then I pour one out for my homey. It. Is. Hard. Sometimes it feels like you are raising Jekyll and Hyde. I think this especially happens with girls because they know exactly what they need to do to please people (speaking from my own experience). The problem is, they usually want to please outside authorities, and they reserve their wrath and independent streak for home. Counselor Sissy Goff reminds me that this is because they feel safe at home, but that doesn't make it any easier to endure.

One day, I took a walk around the neighborhood with my daughter. Some of our best conversations happen while we're moving, whether driving in the car or walking down the road. As we walked, I wanted her to tell me the truth about who she truly is. Is she more herself at home or at school? When does she feel like her truest self? So I asked her, "Where do you feel the most like yourself?" She thought about it for a beat, then said, "While I'm riding horses."

And there it was. The perfect answer. The truth.

She is at peace when she rides.

She is in control, not only of a huge animal, but of herself.

She faces fear head-on and chooses courage.

She is brave.

That's who my daughter is. I may see the hard things. She may bump up against me at times. But she's working out who *she* is. And she sees who she is every time she rides a horse. She knows the truth of who she is, and she spoke it out loud.

That's what I want for us. For all of us. I want us to pay attention to who we are and what we really think, want, and believe. And then I want us to start being ourselves even in the face of fear of judgment or punishment. I want all of us to be brave enough to tell the truth about who we are. Because when we do, we give permission to the children we raise to tell the truth, too.

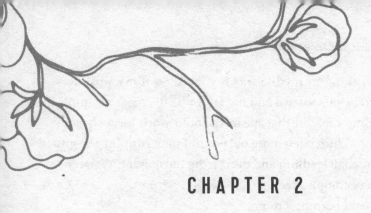

CHAPTER 2

MOTHERHOOD IS A RELATIONSHIP, NOT A CALLING

I began my career after college with a professional minor league baseball team working in their marketing department. Having been a competitive athlete for most of my life, I couldn't imagine a life disconnected from sports. I had loved baseball for as long as I could remember (and if I'm being honest, I secretly wanted to marry a baseball player, so win-win). But I also felt some tension. The job was fun and could potentially afford me a husband (just kidding), but I had been taught that my career needed to be connected to my passion and my purpose—it needed to be meaningful. Could working in baseball really be my purpose? Could it really be meaningful?

I wrestled with these questions because, for me, the most

meaningful thing in my life was my faith. So if my work was supposed to be purposeful and my faith was the most meaningful part of my life, did that mean I should work for a church? Working for a church felt more purposeful than running the gift shop at a baseball stadium and overseeing the mascot. Work and purpose were complicated.

And then I became a mom.

If my career choice felt complicated before, now the tension was really ramped up. I felt like motherhood was purposeful, but I also felt like what I did for churches was purposeful. Now I felt torn between two purposes—my work and motherhood. How was I supposed to pursue both purposes? If work is connected to my purpose, where does motherhood fit in?

There's a word attached to purpose that seems to complicate things. In Christian circles, the term *calling* frequently appears alongside *purpose* and even *work*.

"What are you *called* to do?" Christians commonly ask each other.

In Christian circles, the idea of calling seems to be elevated above everything else. If we feel like something is holy, we label it a calling. Someone is called to be a missionary. Called to be a preacher. Called into full-time ministry. Somehow those jobs feel more holy or spiritual or worthy. I grew up thinking that if the word *calling* was attached to something, it was validated in some way. So, using that logic, it makes sense we would want to attach the word *calling* to motherhood. Because motherhood *is* spiritual. It *is* important. It *is* valuable.

Interestingly, the Bible doesn't talk about motherhood as a calling.

I remember reading books, listening to sermons, and hearing

a consensus that a woman's place—their highest calling, purpose, and passion—was raising their kids *at home*. They were told that finding purpose in work was acceptable until they had the opportunity to raise kids. But ultimately, motherhood was the greatest aspiration.

So if motherhood is the greatest work you could ever do— the highest calling—then is parenting supposed to be my *work*? How do I manage the tension between work and calling? Is being a mother something I *do* rather than something I *am*? Isn't it actually more about a relationship than a job?

If you feel a little nervous about where we're going, let me put you at ease. I value my faith, and I value being a mother, but something about the word *calling* in relation to motherhood rubs me the wrong way. Something about it seems to add unnecessary pressure to parenting.

Somewhere along the line, this topic became divisive. Arguments about whether or not motherhood is a calling are everywhere. In fact, what you believe about motherhood has become, for some, a marker of what kind of Christian you are. But am I really a better Christian, a more spiritual Christian, if I'm a mother and find my purpose in motherhood alone?

An unhealthy division between women who worked and women who stayed home with the kids was created. All of a sudden, we felt like we had to choose a side: stay at home or go to the office. But these two things are very different. It's not a fair comparison.

Let me put my cards on the table here. I don't think motherhood is a vocation. If you hop on ZipRecruiter.com right now, you won't find one single listing for motherhood. It's not a job because you don't get paid for it.

Yet saying that motherhood is not a vocation doesn't diminish its value.

Let's be clear. This isn't an argument about which choice is better. Either choice—staying home or going to work—is honorable. Either choice is valuable. It's just that one is a job and the other isn't.

I can already hear the pages of this book being burnt. But before you light the match, hear me out.

I don't devalue anyone's choice to stay home. Being a stay-at-home mom with kids under age three was the hardest thing I've ever done. Staying home is hard. *It is work*. But just because something is work doesn't make it a job. Motherhood requires work, but it's not a job.

Sometimes we're led to believe that if we want to do more than be a mom, we must be selfish and focused only on self-fulfillment. Sometimes there isn't a choice about jobs. Most of us need them. And I would argue that whether you work for income, work for purpose, or work for pleasure, we are created to work. We will find more joy in life if we find work to do that brings us fulfillment and meaning.

What you do as a writer could bring fulfillment and meaning.

What you do as a tailor could bring fulfillment and meaning.

What you do as an accountant could bring fulfillment and meaning.

What you do as a teacher could bring fulfillment and meaning.

What you do as a scientist could bring fulfillment and meaning.

What you do as a mother could bring fulfillment and meaning.

Being created to work is about finding what brings meaning and keeping that in your life. It doesn't mean that what brings you meaning is your job. And it doesn't mean that what brings you meaning is more biblical or more spiritual than something else. Cheering on the Atlanta Braves can bring you meaning. Crunching numbers can bring you meaning. And changing diapers can bring you meaning. But just because something is meaningful doesn't make it your calling.

Maybe the conversation should center more around *meaning* and less around *calling*.

The very fact that I'm writing an entire chapter about this topic highlights our privilege. I would argue that our version of biblical motherhood is viewed through an American lens. There are mothers in Africa, Iran, and Haiti who love their kids. They provide for their kids. They protect their kids at all costs. But they don't have the privilege of viewing motherhood as their calling and purpose or to choose between working to pay the bills and staying home. Their world isn't centered around creating a perfect place for their kids to experience an Americanized gospel.

In her book *For the Love*, Jen Hatmaker proposes that if something isn't true for the single mom in Haiti, then it isn't true. I think we can adopt that principle in regard to motherhood as a calling. Saying that motherhood is a calling is an American privilege. Not every mother gets that choice. I know many single moms who would love to stay home with their kids—to make raising kids their job—but they can't.

The problem is that when we view raising our kids as our job, we automatically negate those women who don't have a choice to stay home. Without saying it, we diminish their role as mothers. And what about the women who want to have kids more than anything but are unable to? Are they less valuable? Did they miss their ultimate calling? Will they never experience the greatest meaning in life?

The Christian community has elevated staying home with the kids by saying that those who choose to stay home recognize the value of their kids. But wouldn't you say that those who choose to work (or don't have a choice to stay home) also value their kids?

I've read articles that claim that women who choose to work rather than raise kids (which the authors believe must be done as a stay-at-home mom) are seeking self-fulfillment in a selfish way. I've met plenty of working mothers, and none of them view what they do for income as greater than what they do for their kids. In fact, for them the two are actually connected—that is, they work so that they can provide a life for their kids. Just because you have a job outside the home doesn't mean you are being selfish. Staying home (choosing motherhood as the ultimate calling) is a privilege that not every mother can afford.

My relationship with my kids is just that—a relationship. It's not a vocation. Motherhood as a vocation makes as much sense as saying that being married is my vocation.

When I was twenty-six, I met the man I ended up marrying. But there was no magical moment when God called me into marriage. I was never anointed with oil. I never had hands laid on my shoulders during a church service. I simply made a choice. I *chose* to marry Scott Bragg. I chose a relationship.

We see the value in marriage, yet we don't see it as a calling. For some reason, motherhood is viewed differently, even though it's also a relationship. I am a wife. I am a mother. Roles I play. Relationships I have. Responsibilities I hold. You don't have to see something as a calling to appreciate its value and importance.

Being a mom is the hardest thing I have ever done. I have never been more beaten up, spoken down to, dog-tired, and at rock bottom than I have in parenting. It. Is. Hard. Yet I still show up every time. I do this not because I'm called to be a mother. I do this not because it's my job. I show up again and again because I love these humans. I show up because I'm in a relationship with them. I show up because I chose to become a parent.

When you view motherhood as a calling, ultimately you're saying that your role as a mom should be your identity, that it's who you are. And while that role may make up who you are in part, we all know it isn't the full picture. You are more than a mom. You are more than a wife. You are more than an employee. You have an identity that goes beyond those things.

There's a problem with tying our purpose—our identity, our worth—to any specific thing, even if that thing is something as important and meaningful as motherhood. When we tie our worth to a certain role we play, we end up hopping on the struggle bus of never feeling like we are enough. What we do can give us meaning in life, but it was never meant to be what gives us value.

When I read articles that describe motherhood as a calling, all I feel is pressure. Are you laying down your life for your kids? (Have you seen my stretch marks?) Do you respond patiently to their fussiness? Are you pointing them toward the gospel every day? I always seem to answer these types of questions the "wrong" way. I get annoyed with my kids. I often want to choose my own needs over theirs, so call me selfish. When we ask ourselves questions like these, we start to feel like failures. That's what pressure does to us.

Pressure can make us feel like bad moms. We aren't doing enough. We aren't joyful enough. We don't love our kids enough.

(Let's be honest: I love my kids. I'd take a knife for them, but in some moments, I just don't like them. And some people want me to feel guilty for thinking that.)

When I took the pressure off myself by refusing to view motherhood as a calling, I found freedom to be my authentic self with my kids. I was able to tell them when I felt annoyed with them. And do you know what their response was? After considering for a few minutes how this moment of parenting—of being in relationship with them—was hard, they apologized. It wasn't about the gospel. It wasn't about the Romans Road. It was about being human. About allowing them to see what love should look like. About allowing my girls to see the real me and to realize that not everything is easy. That they aren't my sole focus.

We don't have to attach the word *calling* to motherhood in order to value it. I think people want women to feel validated in raising their kids. And I get it—mothering isn't easy. On most days, it isn't fulfilling, and no one is validating my work.

Being a mom is an important role. You carry influence. (Although, if you see my kids' outfit choices, please don't think that is my influence.) What you do as a mother is valuable. Changing diapers. Watching episodes of *Curious George*. Potty training. Teaching a child to ride a bike. Navigating friend drama. Enduring hours of homework. Being the pushing-off point for your teenager. It's all honorable, valuable work. But it is not your calling.

You are free to work, free to find meaning and purpose and pleasure in whatever you do. What you do in life, whether in work or relationships, is valuable. It matters. But don't let whatever you choose to do add pressure to your life. Your calling, your purpose, your meaning is bigger than a relationship, a job, or a role you play.

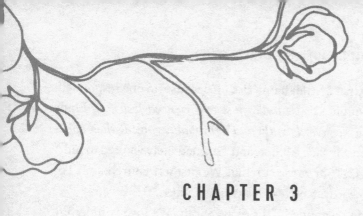

CHAPTER 3

I AM LOVED *BECAUSE* OF WHO I AM, NOT *DESPITE* WHO I AM

Can I just confess something right now before we move on any further?

I cuss. Like, I use four-letter words.

There. I said it. It's out in the open. Don't get me wrong; I do have a fully developed brain, so I know when it's inappropriate to use such language. But living in the South, I'm aware that politeness reigns and people still feel like women should be polite and proper. I guess I've always cussed, but I used to say the words under my breath or in my heart.

So with that in mind, let me tell you a little story.

One night, as I hung out with some friends from church, I let one of those little four-letter words slip. The moment I said it, I immediately felt a little shame rise up because no one responded. *Oh no!* I thought. *These ladies just experienced Jesus, and now I'm throwing cuss words at them. I'm probably ruining their spiritual moment.* My face felt hot, and I immediately wanted to hide. I quickly said, "Sorry for cussing! We just left church, and I'm saying cuss words. Not very Jesus-like, I guess."

Someone responded, "It's okay, Sarah. We love you *despite* the fact that you cuss." Her response was meant to remind me that I am loved, but it felt off. Instead of feeling love, I felt shame. She wasn't intentionally shaming me, but the incident underscores what so many of us believe about ourselves when it comes to love and how we give it. It highlights a belief that we have to do something more to be loved, or act a certain way, or work harder to be loved instead of just being loved. Period.

I went home and cried to my husband, and then I went to work processing why that experience didn't sit well with me. This is how I've learned to deal with emotions like shame. I have to get curious and figure out why I felt that way. Why did my friend's statement feel like a cut? Why did that word, *despite*, carry such weight? As I looked at the situation, I went further back in life. I looked at other moments of rejection, other times when I felt like I hadn't been enough for someone or, conversely, when I'd been *too* much. In all of these instances, the feelings were the same.

As I looked back, I realized that one of my greatest challenges has been believing that I am loved and worthy and enough *as I am.* Maybe it's part of my personality as someone who is hardwired to view performance and achievement as a means of securing value. Maybe it's just part of being female. For whatever reason, I feel like I've spent most of my life giving myself a set of prerequisites for value, for worth, for enoughness.

As a result, I felt I had to perform for my worth. When I walked into a room, I knew what to say, who to speak to, what not to say, *and* what to wear in order to be seen and loved. That's hustling. I learned these skills early because my first major introduction to rejection and shame happened at age nine, when a girl at a pool party called me fat. My physical reaction as a child in that moment was the same reaction I experienced as a grown woman after the cussing incident with my church friends.

I felt embarrassed.

I felt distraught.

I felt lonely.

I felt unaccepted.

So I performed. I performed because I knew that my enoughness, my worthiness, my value were apparently based on something very conditional. I lived and breathed if/then statements.

I'll be worthy of being loved . . .

If I lose ten more pounds

If I can wear size 26 jeans

If I have a pretty face

If I can make important contributions to my field of work

If successful and popular people accept me and promote me

If these successful and popular people want to be my friend

That's a lot of prerequisites—a lot of conditions. Here's the thing about all of my if/then statements: they have the potential to trigger shame in me. Shame is that emotion that causes you to feel like you are so flawed that love and acceptance aren't options for you. It makes you question whether you are even worthy to be loved or accepted. If/then statements require you to be someone you aren't in order to be loved or accepted. *If I do these things, then I'll be loved.* I believed there were conditions for love. One was loved *even though*, not *as is*.

So when my friend used the word *despite*, it raised up in me the belief that I was not actually loved *as is*. However, raising my girls has helped me check that belief. When I look at them, I realize I don't necessarily believe in prerequisites. I don't necessarily believe in conditions. What I believe when I look at my girls is this truth: I am loved *because* of who I am, not *despite* who I am.

I am loved. Period. As is.

In the process of accepting this truth, I had to wrestle with all those if/then statements—all those prerequisites to love. And as I wrestled, I realized that some of my Christian beliefs were wrapped up in prerequisites.

I heard from many Christians that believing I was enough wasn't biblical. They thought believing I was enough somehow diminished Jesus' worth. They said I needed to believe that my worth, my worthiness of love, was derived solely from the fact that Jesus died on a cross for my sin. I spent most of my life believing that humans were deeply sinful, with no good in them, from the beginning. I believed that only a Savior could solve this problem. But even though I had been a "good Christian girl" my entire life, those beliefs didn't sit well with me when I looked at the faces of my daughters. When I looked at them, I didn't see them as full of sin. No, they weren't perfect, but it felt wrong to believe that my girls were totally depraved and the only way they could be worthy of love was for them to see their need for a Savior.

Now, maybe that sounds like heresy to you. I understand, but hear me out. That feeling sat so deep in my soul that I couldn't shake it. I couldn't look at my girls and say that they were loved *if* or *when*. No. They are loved, no ifs or whens. They are loved as is. Right now. No prerequisites. I didn't want my girls to grow up thinking that they had to perform for their worth—even when it came to Jesus. I wanted my girls to live freely and believe they were worthy of love from the very start of their lives.

Isn't that what the author of Genesis affirms? That in the beginning God created the world, including humans, and said it was good? Worthy of love from the beginning? Good from the beginning?

Friend, we have to get to the place where we love ourselves for who we are and others love us for who we are. And it all starts by learning to love yourself. Now, I realize that for many of you, the idea of self-love sounds nearly heretical. I get it. For many years, I thought self-love was some kind of New Age idea. I believed you weren't supposed to love yourself. You were supposed to see how bad you were so that you would see your need for Jesus.

This harmful belief system didn't break down for me until I was in my late twenties. As I wrestled with my ingrained attitudes and beliefs, I started to see the Great Commandment in a new way.

"'You must love the LORD your God with all your heart, all your soul, and all your mind.' This is the first and greatest commandment. A second is equally important: 'Love your neighbor as yourself.'" (Matt. 22:37–39)

Love God and then love your neighbor *as yourself*.

For the first time, I really read those verses. I'm supposed to love God and my neighbor the way I love *myself*. How then is loving yourself unbiblical? The Bible sets it forth plain as day. It's all connected: God, self, others. I love God. I love people. I love myself. If they are all connected in a positive way, it also means that if I don't love myself, then I don't love people and I don't love God. Ouch, right? If we claim to love God but don't love ourselves, are we really loving God?

I had to care about myself the way I cared about others and even about God. And the more I began to love myself, the more I began to love others. The more I showed myself kindness, the more I showed kindness to others. The more I took care of myself, the more a better version of myself showed when I was with others.

Believing that you are enough *as is* does not diminish Jesus in any way. Jesus' death didn't magically give you love or significance or enoughness. His death just revealed what was already true—that you are worthy of the ultimate sacrifice.

No prerequisites needed. No performance required.

When I started practicing self-love, I watched for moments when my prerequisites tried to make an appearance. And when they did, I would call them out for the lies they were. Then I started to change the language I used about myself. In those moments, I would say out loud, "I am loved because of who I am."

The more I practiced speaking compassion to myself, the more I was able to help my girls do the same thing. I would tell them, "I love you because of who you are." And when I heard them speak their own prerequisites, I reminded them that my love includes their big emotions or crooked teeth or shy personality. I spoke truth to the prerequisite.

We can experience those feelings of *despite* in faith, relationships, and even work. Professionally, shame is triggered in me when I feel like my numbers aren't enough. Podcast downloads. Instagram followers. Email subscribers. Someone else always has more, and their more triggers my shame. But I have grown so much in this area.

Just last week, a publicist reached out about promoting a friend's upcoming book to my email subscribers. It was going to be a paid promotion, but the baseline for payment was 10k subscribers. I read that and instantly felt shame because I had far fewer than 10k subscribers. I was not even worthy to get paid to send an email! I started to type my response.

"Thank you for reaching out, but I only have 3k email subscribers."

Then I clicked the delete button over and over until the words were gone because deep in my spirit, I heard a whisper: "Don't speak that shame over yourself. You are worthy because you have 3k subscribers, not only when you have 10k subscribers. You are worthy *now*. You are worthy *because*."

So I crafted a new response:

"Thank you for reaching out. I have 3k followers and would be happy to promote my friend's book."

You are worthy *now*.

You are loved *because* of who you are, not *despite* who you are. If I believe that to be true for my kids, then it is true for me and for you. Imagine if you stopped the hustle. Imagine if you felt free enough or peaceful enough to just show up as yourself, knowing you didn't have to do anything to be loved or valued. Imagine if that list of prerequisites were thrown out the window.

Imagine if you were loved whether you weighed 150 pounds or 250 pounds.

Imagine if you were loved whether you raised successful kids or not.

Imagine if you were loved whether you got the promotion or not.

Imagine if you were loved whether those popular people noticed you or not.

Imagine if you were worthy of being loved from the start of your life not based on prerequisites.

You are worthy of love. You are lovable. As is.

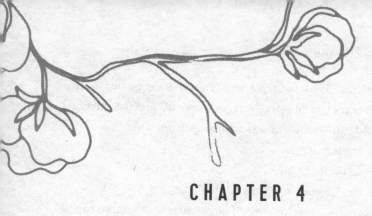

CHAPTER 4

YOU BELONG HERE

Growing up, making friends seemed to be mainly about proximity. When you spend nearly eight hours a day in a classroom together, you're bound to strike up a friendship with someone. Or maybe kids your age lived right next door or down the street. Even siblings were like built-in friendships. When it came to making friends, proximity was king.

For many of us, finding friends became more challenging when we became mothers. I mean, if proximity is an indicator of friendship, then our only option is the baby. And let me just say that while babies are cute, they don't really offer great conversation. I look back at the time when my girls were babies and see that my friendships were fewer. I didn't have the proximity *or* the time to build friendships.

Does that feel familiar to you?

As I look at the faces of women—whether online via social media or face-to-face—I see a commonality emerge. It's a tension every single one of us feels, no matter our race or our socio-economic bracket or the age of our kids. We all feel the tensions that surround our friendships as adults. Bottom line?

Women are lonely.

Women feel out of place.

Women feel unseen and unaccepted.

It's not surprising if this rings true because we spend so much of our lives in isolation. Sure, the cashier at Target saw you today. Or the Starbucks barista chatted with you in the drive-through. But you spend most of your time feeling like people don't really see you or know you. You spend a lot of time wondering if you truly belong somewhere.

I think this tension highlights the fact that motherhood is one of the greatest contributors to loneliness. No one tells you this when you are a new mom. No one tells you how lonely you can feel even when you are actually never alone. Your child is always with you, yet you have never felt more unknown and unseen.

And here's the thing about feeling unknown and unseen: you ultimately feel like you don't belong.

Having people follow us online or know who we are doesn't automatically give us a sense of *belonging*. Having a network of acquaintances provides a place to *fit in*, but there is a difference between fitting in and actually belonging. Think about all the places you go in a single day or week or month and all the groups you find yourself a part of.

Work
School activities
Home
Exercises classes

Church
Gatherings with friends

Think about who you are in those places with those people. Would you say the people you know really know you? I would argue that most of the time we have learned how to *fit in*. It's not much different than what we experienced as middle schoolers or high schoolers. We know what to do and how to act and what to say in order to be accepted into a certain group of people.

So why do we leave that group or that place and still feel empty—like we weren't completely seen or fully understood? Or like we were simply doing a dance or playing a part?

It's because we were simply fitting in. We didn't experience belonging. Belonging is showing up as you are and finding acceptance. Belonging is showing up the way you are, whether you're in a state of stress, grief, or even joy. It's being able to share an honest story of your life and find compassion on the other side. But finding this kind of belonging is often difficult at this age and stage of life.

Fitting in is easier than belonging. Sometimes it's easier to put on a smile even if you feel terrible. Sometimes it's easier to fake being happy about something in front of others. Sometimes it's easier to hide who you really are in order to be liked. Brené Brown says, "Fitting in is one of the greatest barriers to belonging. Fitting in is all about assessing a situation and becoming who you need to be in order to be accepted. Belonging, on the other hand, doesn't require us to *change* who we are; it requires us to *be* who we are."[1] We can fit in with a group because we all have third-grade girls at the same school, or we can fit in with a group online because we're all interested in the same thing. But real belonging goes deeper, and I think that's why we still feel lonely even though we may have three thousand "friends" on social media. We confuse belonging with fitting in.

Fitting in for me looks like:

Agreeing to like something I don't (going to an event when I'd rather stay home)

Dressing a certain way to match the group (stressing about not wearing the current trends)

Aligning with certain ideologies in order not to rock the boat (saying I agree when I don't)

Making decisions based on FOMO instead of what I really want to do (and doing this on my kids' behalf too)

Playing along (not speaking up when I know I should)

Denying who I really am in order to be liked (deciding my true self is too much or not enough)

Sometimes, in relationships, fitting in is about meeting certain criteria in order to be accepted.

You have to dance the dance.

Wear the clothes.

Talk the talk.

Pretend to like the things or believe the things.

This happens all the time. For many Christians, church is supposed to be a place where you find belonging. However, in many churches and groups of Christians, you have to believe certain things, say certain things, and even vote a certain way. And if you don't, then you don't belong. So we talk the talk. We dance the dance. We do what we need to do and say what we need to say, thinking we'll find belonging, but all we're actually doing is fitting in.

I think we do this—I'm speaking from experience here—because we are afraid that the core of who we are makes us unworthy of belonging in that group. If we truly were our authentic selves, we don't think they would allow us in the group. So we let our desire to fit in outweigh our need to be our authentic selves.

Can I just say that I'm tired?

Fitting in can be exhausting and often only perpetuates the sense of loneliness we feel. When it comes to building a tribe of people and finding friends who accept you, fitting in is simply not enough.

One of the things our family is working on is cultivating a sense of belonging. Your family is your first opportunity of belonging, your most important and primal social group. It should be your safest place. Our girls will go through seasons when they don't belong with different groups, but we hope they will always feel like they belong at home. This may sound easy, but it's not. It's not easy because we are humans living in a home with other humans who are all different.

Every day, before our girls get out of the car to walk into school, my husband has started saying something that we hope lays the foundation of belonging. He says, "Remember, you are loved no matter what you do, say, or think." Love is the essence of belonging. We hope our girls will remember this truth when they make a mistake—big or small. Or when they choose to believe something different from us. Or when they make a choice we wouldn't make. We hope that at the end of the day, no matter what they've done, said, or thought, they will believe that they are loved at home—that they belong at home. We all deserve to be accepted as we are—especially at home.

When I considered how much I want my girls to feel like they belong in our family, I realized I was still afraid of not belonging in my own family. Even as a grown woman, I found myself anxious about not belonging in the family I grew up in. I realized that when my fear of not belonging rises, I start to talk the talk and dance the dance in order to fit in. I find myself holding back my opinions and not saying what I really think. I know what keeps the peace, so instead of revealing more of my real self, I choose not to rock the boat.

For a long time, I was afraid to show up as me. I believed that in order to be accepted, I had to be just like the tribe, the family I belonged to. I had to vote the same way. Believe the same things. Hold the same interests. Raise kids the same way. Engage in the same activities. But as I grew up, I evolved and changed, and I was afraid that the girl who evolved wouldn't be loved the same as the girl who once was.

Raising my girls has highlighted this fear because I want more than anything for them to be able to show up as who they are, even if they act different from me, believe different from me, or vote different from me. I don't want them to settle for a cheaper version of belonging. If I want that for my girls, then why wasn't I willing to want it for myself? The short answer is fear. I was afraid I would be rejected. I was afraid I would disappoint my family. I was afraid they were too fragile to handle the change.

I was settling for a false sense of acceptance.

In 2018, I knew it was time to start letting go of fitting in. It started by discovering who I really am. I lived far too long (and I'm still a work in progress) changing who I was in order to be liked and accepted. A year later, my goal was to be and live out my authentic, real self. I had done the work to figure out who I am, but now it was time to put it out there. That wasn't (and still isn't) always easy. And 2020? That was the year of saying more, speaking up more, and believing I would find belonging because of who I am.

I'm learning that I would rather have fewer friends if it means those friends know and accept me for who I am. I'm learning that I want my family to know the truest version of myself. And when I started to share the truest version of me to the people who mean the most to me, I was met with love.

So how do you find where you can belong?

Here's what has helped me figure out my safe people—people with whom I can be my authentic self, people with whom I can belong. I ask myself these questions:

Do they judge other people's stories?
Do I feel better about myself after spending time with them?
Did they ask me questions or only talk about themselves the whole time?
Do they add value to my life?
Do they show up again and again, no matter what I say or do or think?

This process takes trial and error. Sometimes it feels very risky. But pursuing belonging is part of cultivating a full life. It's a life that Jesus described as *abundant* in John 10:10: "I have come that they may have life, and have it to the full." Life was never meant to be lived in isolation. Nothing good comes from isolation. We were created to connect. It is hardwired into our humanness.

So take a step. Initiate a conversation. Explore opportunities around you. When I started to live out a truer version of myself, I decided to make an effort to spend more time with people who make me feel like I can be my authentic self. I reached out to these people and invited them to have dinner or coffee or go for a walk with me. There is power in invitation. It's always fun to be on the receiving end of an invitation, but sometimes we have to make the first move.

What about creating a sense of belonging at home?

Maybe you feel like you have a place to belong, but you feel the need to foster a sense of belonging in your home for your kids. I wonder if the goal in parenting isn't to raise perfect, well-behaved, well-educated kids, but instead, to raise kids who feel worthy of love, who feel like they belong, who feel like they matter. This might start with asking questions, especially if you have older kids. Ask them if they feel like they belong at home. Depending on the response, maybe an apology is what needs to come next. Figure out how you can be accepting of who they are. And know this won't always be easy. My twelve-year-old has said that I'm trying to make her just like me. That's painful. It's not totally true, but there is some truth in it. I am working on letting her belong as is.

Life is too short to spend our time hustling for acceptance. I would hate to get to the end of my life and realize that no one truly knew who I was and I never really belonged. So let's make a commitment together. We will do the work to accept ourselves for who we are. We will do the work to accept others for who they are. And we will do the work to cultivate a sense of love and belonging.

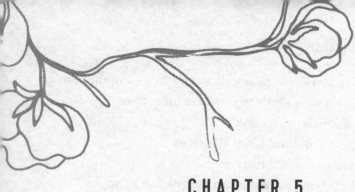

CHAPTER 5

WHAT MADE YOU SMILE TODAY?

One thing I love about children is their absolute ability to be happy. It doesn't take much to make them smile. My neighbor has a one-year-old who immediately smiles whenever she sees me. It's like she's been watching and waiting for me to simply look in her direction, and then when I do, her whole face lights up. That expression of sheer delight is, to me, the epitome of happiness.

Give them a cookie. Happy.

Say yes to jumping on the trampoline. Happy.

Sit down to play dolls. Happy.

Read a bedtime story. Happy.

But I've also found that as easy as it is to make children happy, it is just as easy to make them unhappy. I've been amazed at how quickly the mood can change in our house. My girls can go from zero to sixty on the emotion scale in an instant. One minute they're happy, and the next they're miserable.

Say no to a cookie. Miserable.

Have to go to bed. World War III-status.

Have to take a shower. Life is over.

Raising these humans has shown me how much we need joy and happiness in our lives. I want to smile more. I want to appreciate the small things, the ordinary moments, like little kids do. In those early years of parenting, when life was turned upside down by the arrival of kids, I struggled to find joy in those little, ordinary moments. No matter how much I prayed for joy, I just didn't seem to feel it.

While reading Brené Brown's book *The Gifts of Imperfection*, I started to connect some dots about joy. She is a firm believer (based on research) that joy is connected to gratitude. I found this interesting because she didn't say that if you just pray, joy will follow, or if you just ask for joy, it will show up. She made the critical connection linking joy with gratitude. If you want to be more joyful and experience more happiness, then gratitude is your path. But work is involved.

Can I be honest?

I had never thought about gratitude beyond Thanksgiving. I mean, that's the one time each year we give gratitude the microphone, right? But daily? I hadn't thought about it. I had tried in years past to write down things I was thankful for, and generally, after I got to toilet paper, I couldn't think of anything else. The effort didn't stick until I realized gratitude's connection to joy. I desperately wanted more joy in my life.

Brené Brown says that gratitude is not just an attitude; it's a practice.[1] Her research showed that practicing gratitude leads to joy. If we want to smile more, enjoy life more, experience joy more, then we need to start practicing gratitude.

Here's what that looks like practically for me.

For the past several years, I've made a habit of sitting down every morning with my favorite journal. (I'm a big fan of the Moleskine journals with pages of graph squares instead of lines. There's just something about those tiny squares.) In the top line of squares, I'd write the simple phrase "Thankful for . . ." Then I'd think back to the day before.

What made me smile?

What made me happy?

What was hard but I survived?

Then I'd write down my answers. I didn't put a goal on it, like one thousand things. The goal was just to do this simple practice every day. I wanted to see if there truly was a link, a connection, between gratitude and joy.

After several months of this practice, someone close to me noticed something different in me. As we were talking, she said, "I've noticed for the last few weeks that you seem happy." That was it. Evidence. There truly was a connection between gratitude and joy. Because, you see, I'd started to look around. I'd started to notice the little things, to pay attention to what was happening. The items on my gratitude list were things like coffee and sunshine and great sex and walks with friends and happy hours with neighbors. Simple things. Small things. Yes, sometimes the list included big moments like book deals and podcast guests, but the ordinary things far outnumbered the extraordinary.

It's a proven principle that when you do things over time, you see results. That's why people who work out consistently see a difference in their bodies. Or why people who practice an instrument daily see improvement.

But the phrase, "over time" isn't easy for someone like me. My personality loves efficiency and productivity. I value doing things quickly. Often, this was related to work, but I realized I also wanted quick results for my mental health (not to mention wanting to lose ten pounds in four hours). I wanted to be happy, to find joy in where I was in life, but I wanted it right then. I expected to count my blessings for two days and see the results.

Maybe when I have more followers, I'll be happy.
Maybe when my podcast reaches a million downloads, I'll
    be happy.
Maybe when I have the unreachable guest on my show, I'll
    be happy.
Maybe when I finally get that book deal, I'll be happy.
Maybe when I'm one of the most popular people in my
    field, I'll be happy.

It was like happiness was always slightly out of reach and fully dependent on someone else. But when I started practicing gratitude—focusing on what was already in front of me—something began to shift in me. I started finding happiness in what I was doing in the exact moment that I was doing it. I found joy in not needing to be the most popular or the most recognized. I was finally able to stop attaching happiness to the extraordinary.

It was an interesting feeling. Yes, there was peace, but there was grief, too. I had been striving for so long that letting go felt sad. It was a paradox, a mix of grief at not accomplishing the dream but relief at letting go. The grief wasn't destructive, though, because of the muscle of gratitude I'd been flexing.

Over time, the daily practice of noticing the ordinary around me brought a great sense of peace, joy, and happiness and slowly created a change in me.

That's when I started to consider my girls. Yes, when children are little, happiness is around nearly every corner (unless you decide to limit their cookies). But as they grow older, they start to become more like us and happiness is harder to come by. I wanted to figure out a way to help my girls cultivate more joy in their lives. And from my own experience, I knew the answer was gratitude.

One of the greatest privileges of hosting a podcast is getting to have conversations with absolutely amazing people. I've been fortunate to have America's Supernanny, Dr. Deborah Tillman, join me on the podcast a couple of times. In our first conversation, she talked about the need to teach our kids gratitude. I'd always felt like joy and happiness were difficult concepts to teach children. But Dr. Tillman gave me a great idea. She suggested that when I tuck my girls in at night, I ask them, "What made you smile today?" That is basically what I'm asking myself in the mornings during my own gratitude practice. I know gratitude is connected to happiness and joy, but my girls don't understand that yet. My hope is that the practice of asking them this question will help them get to the point where they begin to ask it of themselves.

Joy is a choice. It happens when we choose to practice it daily. It doesn't happen because we ask for it to be handed to us or poured out on us. It happens when we cultivate it. I remember one day when I woke up and simply felt grumpy. Nothing specific had happened to put me in this frame of mind. I was just there. But I knew happiness wasn't just going to surface. I was going to have to help it appear. So I sat down with my journal and began writing down all the things that made me smile, all the things I could be grateful for. I sometimes believe that simply taking action moves you forward. In this instance, the act of writing things down moved me forward.

Finding happiness takes action, practice, and persistence.

As I write this chapter, we are knee-deep in quarantine due to COVID-19. One thing that has helped me remain sane has been taking walks. In fact, some days I take up to four walks! I just need to get out to move and think. And probably like many of you, I listen to podcasts when I walk. I recently listened to Dax Shepard interview Will Arnett on the *Armchair Expert* podcast. Dax told Will he was one of the most positive-minded people he knew and asked him why. Will said that if you change your mind, you change your life. That what you think about has the power to color how you see your life. He said, "If I think on the lack of something, then I get a lack of something."[2] Isn't that profound? If I'm always thinking of what is lacking, then I see life as lacking.

My personality type always tends to see what is lacking— there is always more to do, more to achieve, never enough. People call this a scarcity mindset. It is a limiting belief that says there is never enough. For instance, I used to be the kind of person who, upon waking up in the morning, would proclaim I hadn't gotten enough sleep. (Full disclosure: I still struggle to refrain from doing this.) Scarcity. I would think about the day ahead and feel like I didn't have enough time to do it all. Scarcity. And you know what? At the end of the day, I confirmed that to be true. I was tired. I hadn't completed the entire list. *If I think on the lack of something, then I get a lack of something.*

One day as I walked with my dear friend Lesley, I poured out my woes. I was having a particularly relentless woe-is-me day—or as my mom used to call it, a pity party. I lamented about work—how no one was sharing the podcast, which meant my social channels weren't growing, which in turn was making me feel blah about myself. The pity party continued as I talked about how discouraged I was that we were still renting and how the housing market was so insane in our area that we would never find a home to buy. Honestly, I'm shocked Lesley was still walking with me even though I'd just buried her in my misery. She politely said, "I always tell my girls when they are spiraling that what you think about is what you get." I knew that to be true, yet when it came to work and home (and let's face it, relationships and myself), I often lived with a scarcity mindset.

Never enough.

Lacking.

Things will always be this hard.

My situation will never work out.

I would look at my life and, perhaps not surprisingly, it confirmed the scarcity. If you are looking for something, you will find it. Every day, I noticed how people shared other podcasts but not mine. Every day I would see others buying homes when we couldn't. Every day I would search for the scarcity in my own life. And every day I would find it.

Do you know what I did after really noticing this negative tendency of mine? I started writing down the positive, the good, in an attempt to change my mindset.

I have enough.

I am enough.

The world isn't against me.

Everything will work out at some point.

The scarcity mindset is evident in my kids, too. It's just so easy to expect the worst—maybe because we fear being let down. But the more we can teach our kids to weed the scarcity from their minds, the happier and more joyful they will be.

Practicing gratitude didn't only change the way I viewed work and rest; it also changed how I see my girls. When I began to notice the things that made me smile, I found my demeanor changing toward them. Instead of focusing on what they lacked (scarcity), I made note of the good. I wrote it down and said it out loud. How we think is how we live.

So, how do you want to live?

Imagine if you started to see the beauty, the good, the fullness of what you have and where you are in life. Imagine the expression that would appear on your face. Imagine the fullness you would feel. If you want more joy, more happiness, in your life, it begins with gratitude. Day in and day out, pay attention to what makes you smile and write it down. And over time, I believe you'll notice a little more joy in your heart.

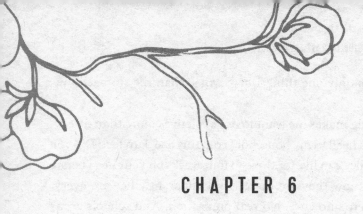

CHAPTER 6

BE BRAVE

I'm going to mention two words that will make you immediately cringe or crawl for safety. These two words have been known well by mothers of all generations. But they aren't words I gave much attention to until I was a mother.

Stomach bug.

There. I said it. I will do nearly anything to prevent this plague from touching my home and my children. I am willing to anoint everyone with oil, cut out sugar, and drink nothing but bone broth to prevent the stomach bug. Maybe even take daily baths in bleach. I remember one Thanksgiving celebration when half of the attendees fell victim to the bug. My brother, who fries our turkey every year, decided it was a good idea to cook the turkey while under the influence of the stomach bug—without our knowledge. We'll never know if this was his way of instituting a full-court takeover of the family throne or just simple neglect (likely the latter).

There's only one thing I hate worse than the stomach bug. Lice.

Nothing makes me want to use expletives more than discovering that a head in my household contains lice. Fun fact: Did you know that lice can live for three to four weeks on your head before you even know they are there? And apparently lice are everywhere. There's no cure. No real prevention. And schools aren't even required to tell you there's been an outbreak. Life is over.

I open this chapter with these awful ailments not to get you to close the book and never return, nor to encourage you to immediately go check your kid's head for lice (although that is a really good idea). My goal here is to bring up the idea of things that are contagious.

Contagious is a word we mothers are well aware of. And just like the stomach bug is contagious, positive things can be contagious. One of these things is courage. In fact, I didn't know courage was contagious until I became a mom. I truly had never thought much about courage before.

I grew up playing the piano in front of hundreds of people. That required courage.

I moved across the country knowing no one when I was twenty-one years old. That required courage.

I took a chance on getting published when I was only twenty-five. That required courage.

In the moment, I didn't think about any of these actions as being courageous. But looking back, I see how brave I was.

I'm sure I could list a lot of other things I've done that required courage, but nothing compares to the amount of courage it takes to parent. It has been the most courageous thing I've ever done. To me, parenting feels like *The Hunger Games*. In those movies, it's all about survival. At all costs. You do what you have to do to make it out of there alive. Surviving equals winning. That is exactly what parenting is like, and I've been chosen as the tribute. I walk out on the field every day and try to survive. But just because I walk out on the field doesn't mean I'm not afraid. Most days, I'm afraid. Most days, I'm scared out of my mind.

Will my kids turn out okay?

Will they be rejected?

Will they find friends?

Will they make a choice that completely derails their future?

Will I know how to handle this?

Will they pass middle school?

But just because I'm scared doesn't mean I shouldn't walk forward. I always think about fear and courage in light of my kids. Sometimes my girls say they're afraid of going to sleep. Do you think I just say, "Oh no! Since you're afraid, maybe you should just stay up all night"? No way! They still have to sleep. (And *I* still need them to sleep.) They have to find a way to sleep even though they feel afraid. Or, if they were scared to cross the street, I wouldn't just give in and say, "Well, I guess we'll never see the other side." That's crazy! I would take their hand, and we'd walk across the street together. That's courage.

Nothing is more vulnerable—nothing feels more uncertain, more unknown, more perilous—than parenting. That's why we need to have courage. Parenting gives us the opportunity to realize how brave we actually are.

My dear friend, Sissy Goff, is a bestselling author and phenomenal counselor. I have her on speed dial and have called many times so she can walk me through one situation or another with my girls. Sissy wrote a book for tween girls called *Braver,*

Stronger, Smarter, which is a companion to her book for parents, *Raising Worry-Free Girls*. I can hear her wise voice over and over again in my head: "You are braver, stronger, and smarter than you think you are." We can be brave. We can be strong. We can be smart. We can have the courage to keep showing up day after day and to face our fears.

When you do anything over and over, it begins to sink in. The more you practice something, the more you figure it out and the more you become what you want to be. So when you practice courage over and over, you begin to become braver. You learn to swim by swimming. You learn to cook by cooking. You learn to drive by driving. Let's use the same logic with courage. You learn to be courageous by being courageous—by "couraging."

When you surround yourself with wise, brilliant people, you can take what they dish out and apply it straight to your own life. For me, one of those people is my friend Sarah Anderson. In fact, she was one of my very first guests on *Surviving Sarah*.[1] In that episode, she talked about how she tells her boys to be kind, be wise, and be brave. So I took those phrases and started saying them to my girls. I began challenging them to be brave every day at school but in ways they maybe hadn't thought about before. I wanted them to know that bravery looks like raising your hand to ask a question. It looks like sitting next to a kid who is all alone, even though your other friends won't join you. It looks like swinging by yourself on the playground. That's courage. That's bravery. And the more I coached them on what being brave looks like, the more I realized that I needed to be brave in my own life.

Raising girls has made me lean into my own fears and discover my own courage in ways I never imagined. I've started doing things that make me nervous, that raise my blood pressure, that may result in failure. I was talking to the girls about writing this book and Rory asked why I was doing it when it might fail. I told her it's good to lean in when you feel afraid. It's good to prove to yourself that you are braver than you think you are. And do you know what happens when you keep couraging? You build resilience. You discover you can handle more than you think you can. You develop the grit you need to persevere.

Nothing has taught me more about courage and resilience and grit than watching Sinclair ride horses. I remember one particular lesson that nearly scarred me for life. Sinclair was in the jumping portion of her lesson and the jumps that day were around two feet high. As she cantered toward the final jump with the momentum of already having cleared two jumps, the horse came to a dead stop and Sinclair went straight over the horse's head and the jump. I held myself back from running into the arena. I had to allow her trainer to deal with the situation. It was very important for Sinclair to get back on the horse and do it again; otherwise the horse would think it could throw her again. As I watched ten-year-old Sinclair saddle up and face the same jump again, I saw grit and determination. She developed deeper courage by couraging. That's how we all need to approach life.

Developing courage by couraging may look like:

Saying "I'm sorry" to your child or partner
Having a hard conversation
Drawing boundaries
Wearing the swimsuit
Dancing like no one's watching

Taking a new job

Moving to a new city

Learning something new

With every step of courage, you become more courageous. Yes, being brave will require facing the unknown and the scary. It will require going forward even though the outcome is uncertain. I can't think of a better word to describe parenting (and really life in general) than *wilderness*. The wilderness is the perfect image of something unknown, scary, and uncharted. Charles Lindbergh said, "Real freedom lies in wilderness, not in civilization." Maybe freedom is found when we are braving the wilderness of parenting—when we are facing the unknown but also showing up with courage. And maybe freedom is found when we take the opportunity to raise ourselves even while we are raising our kids.

Just like the stomach bug is contagious, so is courage. When you choose to show up, other people find courage. When you show up in the middle of the hard, others gain courage to be brave. When you show up with honesty, others gain courage to be honest. Your courage doesn't breed judgment but brings about solidarity with others.

I see you, sister. I see you slumped over in the Target aisle while your kid is having a meltdown on the floor. I see you when you are on the verge of tears. I see you when your kid breaks your heart. I want to choose courage so that you can choose courage. We can do this together. We can survive this together.

Every time you speak up, step out, or show up, you are choosing courage. With each courageous step, you are writing a braver story. Be brave, friend. Your courage is contagious.

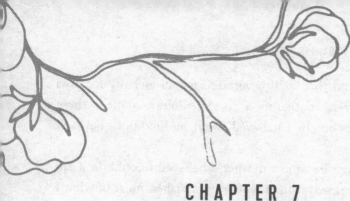

CHAPTER 7

YOU CAN'T HAVE IT ALL

When we were young, we believed a lot of lies. It makes sense why—we hadn't experienced enough life yet for certain things to come into question.

For instance . . .

We believed a magic fairy exchanged our teeth for money. My younger daughter believed in the tooth fairy so much that she would write her a letter filled with questions every time she lost a tooth.

We believed a fat man dressed in red delivered gifts at Christmas.

Don't even get me started on the Easter Bunny.

As we grew older, we believed other lies, like money would come easily, unwanted pounds could melt away in just seven days, and love is blind.

We believe other lies when we become a mother. We believe our child will be an angel, that they will do exactly what we want them to do, and that we'll be praised for all eternity for how amazing we are at motherhood. As ridiculous as some of these sound, there is one lie I believed about motherhood that isn't quite so silly.

When I first became a mother, I believed I could do it all. I was a determined woman who accomplished most of what I put my mind to. But the thing about motherhood is that it isn't something to be accomplished, figured out, or even completed. Raising kids isn't like that. And it happens to most of us at a time when we are also building our careers. Which is why the lie that we can do it all is so appealing. We hold the new baby in our arms while firmly believing we can make it happen.

We have bills to pay.

We have dreams and ambitions.

And we want to give this baby the best we have to offer. We want them to feel our presence. We want them to know we care. We want to be the one to meet all their needs.

So the story we tell ourselves, the lie we believe, is that we can do it all. We think we can be fully present with our kids at all times and also present for work during work hours. And because of the wonder of technology, I believe more and more women will be afforded the opportunity to try to do both.

Now, let me explain what I mean by *both*. I was afforded the opportunity to continue working full-time but from home while obviously being a full-time mom. I could "have it all"—or so I thought. I had painted a picture in my head of how this new job would work. I'd wake up early to the smell of coffee and crank out words on a page before the babe woke. Then, while she was awake, she would sit beside me in a bouncy seat or lie on the ground on a playmat while I continued the endeavor of writing all the words. While she napped anywhere from two to three hours at a stretch, I would work in overdrive, making sure to complete everything. Being both a full-time mom and a full-time employee seemed possible, doable—even easy.

I'm hoping that those of you who have also attempted this feat cracked a smile as you read that last paragraph. Maybe you even snorted out the coffee you were sipping. I can imagine you wanting to shake your head and cup my face and say, "Sweet girl."

Spoiler alert: It didn't go as planned. Not even close.

I had no energy to wake up early because I was up all night feeding the baby or sleep training. She never wanted to be without me. I could be in the shower with her sitting in the bouncy seat in front of the shower and she would scream the whole time. And naptime? I learned very quickly that you couldn't count on it. Some days she slept like a charm. Other days, she slept forty-five minutes before screaming. Working while she was up was out of the question. I couldn't even connect words to form sentences. It felt like my career as a writer was over.

Apparently, I couldn't have it all.

Here's the thing: I wanted it all. I didn't want to say no to anything. I didn't want to miss out on anything. I wanted to keep my job the same. I loved my job. I wanted to believe that I really could continue to do everything I'd done before having a kid while working from home. But I didn't want to sacrifice anything on the home front either. I wanted to be fully present for my daughter. I had read too many books about how important it is for moms to raise their kids. I wrestled with so much shame around choosing to work versus choosing to stay home. So I chose both, which led to full-time frustration and full-time disappointment.

I don't believe that motherhood comes naturally to everyone.

It certainly didn't for me. Being a mother is the most unnatural, natural thing you can do. No one knows how to actually give birth, what to do about diaper rash, or why kids require so much stuff. Don't even get me started on breastfeeding! Talk about something that feels unnatural but is totally natural.

I felt like doing it all—working full-time and raising my daughter full-time—would prove that I was truly cut out for doing it all. But it only highlighted the opposite. It wasn't working, which made me believe that I was either not a good writer or not a good mom. On some days I believed both. If I was a good mom, I could figure this out. If I was a good writer, I could still string words together to form sentences even on minimal sleep.

When we believe some women are just naturally better at being mothers, we set ourselves up for failure. We set ourselves up for disappointment. We set ourselves up to experience shame.

I sat in the middle of the tension: I wanted to go to work, and I wanted to stay home. I didn't want to give up anything. I kept trying to force myself to have it all.

I longed to contribute to the world. People would say, "But, Sarah, you are contributing to the world by raising her." *Shame.*

Other people would say, "Sarah, maybe you should be a working mom." *Shame.*

In my mind, being a working (not from home) mom was just not on the table for me. Even my husband encouraged me to stay home with the baby. He wanted me to be happy, and he saw the way I felt torn and just wanted to fix it. I understand that, but his input just added to the shame.

To be fair, I couldn't imagine a life in which I wasn't with this kid all the time. Besides what I kept hearing from church and culture, the reality was that I felt jealous about my time with her. I couldn't imagine dropping her off at daycare. But I also couldn't imagine quitting my job. I wasn't willing to sacrifice. Being a mom required more sacrifice than I'd imagined. Sure, I knew I'd have to sacrifice sleep, but even with that, I thought it would only be for the first few months. Who knew I'd still be sacrificing sleep with a twelve-year-old?

I was trying to do it all and wasn't doing anything well. I felt completely torn. You know the principle in budgeting that every yes is a no to something else? If I want to buy this sweater, then that's a no to the shoes. We understand this principle in finances, but it's harder to figure out with our time, our work, and our kids.

Now, I'm not saying you are negating your opportunity to parent by working or vice versa. I'm saying that when we try to say yes to everything, then frustration, disappointment, and discontentment will follow.

When Sinclair was in first grade, I'd finally started to accept the reality that I couldn't have it all. I'd started to weigh my choices, to give myself appropriate expectations. So when a work opportunity came up, I knew that if I wanted to remain at home with Rory, who was a preschooler, I could only manage working in a part-time capacity. It was a sacrifice, but setting myself up with a realistic expectation gave me freedom and peace.

Each of us needs to figure out what works best for ourselves and our families. If you choose to work full-time outside the home, great. If you choose to stay home full-time, great. If you choose to come up with a different type of work-and-motherhood concoction, great. You get to decide what works best for you. You get to decide what will give you peace.

Raising kids is stressful, so do anything you can to relieve the pressure. I often look back and wish I'd accepted the fact that motherhood would be hard no matter what I chose. I wish that I'd believed my girls would be okay going to daycare. I wish I'd told myself that sacrifice would be required, and it would be okay. When you say yes to working full-time, you can't say yes to staying home with your child full-time. There just aren't enough hours in the day for that.

Whatever works best for you and your family is the best option. Also, the fact that this was even a discussion on the table for our family shows our privilege. So many women don't have the opportunity to wrestle with this choice.

I wanted to be a mom who was present with my child whenever she was awake. I didn't want to use the TV as a babysitter. I wanted to be the mom who took her to the park and showed up at all her school functions. I wanted the door of our home to be open for playdates with all the neighborhood kids. I wanted to be perceived as laid-back, someone who wasn't bothered by all the chaos that comes with motherhood.

I also wanted to be the writer who wrote amazing stories, who could see the world in a way that inspired and encouraged others. I wanted to meet all the people and have all the conversations. I wanted to chase down all the ideas.

The image of the mother I'd intended to be never came to fruition. And all my dreams as a writer and creator didn't come to fruition either. I learned that I can't have it all. But that's okay.

Balancing it all is a myth. It's a beautiful lie that we tell ourselves and hear from others in order to help us cope with the pace and expectations of life. In different seasons of life and motherhood, sacrifice will be required. The sacrifice will look like saying yes to one thing while saying no to something else.

Choices. Concessions. Limitations. Every day, life is full of them. Yet somehow, I felt like I was exempt. I felt like I didn't need to make a choice or limit myself. I would tell my girls that they couldn't have it all, but why did I think I could have it all in my own life?

It's easy to look at other women and assume that it's possible to do it all. I can hop onto social media and see how some women seem to be able to work, be fully present with their kids, and even have a side hustle going. But as I look around my house and at myself, I know that scenario just doesn't ring true.

I realized I was a forty-year-old woman with elementary-age expectations from life. I wanted to have all the things, do all the things, and miss out on nothing. I basically wanted Cheetos and Oreos all day, every day, just like my girls. I wanted to leave my towels on the floor and have someone else pick them up. But what is true for my girls is true for me—I can't have it all.

If there is one thing I want to say to moms—new moms especially—it's that you can't have it all. That statement doesn't have to be a negative one. It can be a freeing one. When I allow myself to accept that I can't have it all, peace follows. I'm forced to make some choices, but that's not bad.

Let me pause and tell you a little story about making choices. One of my kids' favorite things to do is go inside a convenience store while we are getting gas on a road trip. We don't buy candy or chips from a gas station unless we're on a road trip, so it's sort of a big deal to my kids. On this particular trip, Sinclair wanted some candy. But the problem was that she had to choose between M&M's and sour candy. She couldn't have both. And this decision absolutely tanked her. She couldn't bear the thought of leaving one behind. Her distress rose to the point where she was not only crying but also lying down *on the floor of the convenience store*. I made eye contact with the cashier, and his face said it all. Shock. Concern. Judgment.

I tell you this story because sometimes, making a choice isn't easy. Sinclair was behaving like we've all wanted to behave when faced with an impossible choice. Letting go of one thing to have another is hard. But sometimes we have to do it.

We are confronted with this belief in so many areas of life. This belief that we can have it all makes it nearly impossible to make a choice. On some level, I completely relate to my daughter lying in a state of angst and indecision on the convenience store floor.

When it comes to where I live, I want it all. I want to live in the quaint downtown community, send my kids to an amazing public school, keep my friends and family close by, and have a big house with land for horses and a pool out back. Oh, and if I can have the beach, that would be great too. The problem is that in order to have all these things, I would have to make way more money than I currently make. Also, a yes to some of these things means a no to others. I may want it all, but it's impossible to have it all.

I thought I could be fully employed and fully a mom—all at home. But after trying to do it all, I finally made some choices. I decided to cut my work hours. I figured I could work ten to fifteen hours a week from home but not forty. Then, when my work hours needed to increase, I made another choice. I hired a nanny for two days a week. I wanted to be the mom who could be fully present at home with her kids and also meet every deadline, but it just wasn't working. Hiring a nanny so I could go to an office to work two days a week felt like a concession, but it needed to happen.

And right now, during the worldwide pandemic? I can't have it all. I've cleared all excess projects off my to-do list. Right now, I can only work on what are "must happen" items.

What does it look like to make concessions? To accept limitations?

Saying no sometimes
Asking for help
Bringing store-bought cookies to a party
Not dieting during a worldwide pandemic
Hiring a nanny
Cutting back hours
Not being a room mom
Signing up for a food delivery subscription
Hiring someone to clean your house or take care of your
    yard

It's okay not to have it all. It's okay not to be able to do it all. You aren't Superwoman. You are human. Different seasons carry different priorities. A yes to one thing inevitably brings a no to something else. The choice usually isn't as easy as deciding which chips to eat for lunch. But you *can* do hard things. And your yes or no to one thing doesn't determine whether you are a good mom or not.

All of those years, I thought parenting was either/or. Either work or stay at home. But in reality, it wasn't about that at all. It was about being present wherever you are. Parenting is about staying engaged, paying attention, and being mentally and emotionally present wherever you are physically present.

You see, you can't have it all—and that's okay. In fact, you likely tell your kids that all the time. But it's true for you, too. Life is full of choices, and some of those choices will feel painful. They will feel like sacrifice. But remember, what your child needs is your engagement, your presence. Your presence in their lives is the win. Lean in to whatever decision you make and then show up, engage, and be present wherever you are.

CHAPTER 8

SHOWING UP IS ENOUGH

I have always been a very competitive person. Growing up, I treated everything like a competition. (I know, annoying. I was that kid.) I always had to beat my brother to the car or behave better or get higher grades. I even viewed going to the dentist as a competition. Whoever had the fewest cavities won! Every time my family played miniature golf, I cried if I lost. (I may or may not have thrown a golf club across the green once.) I wanted to win. That's probably why I played sports all my growing-up years. I played basketball and tennis and did cheer-leading. I didn't play to have fun—I played to win.

My competitive nature didn't just stick to the court. It carried over into other areas of my life. I wanted to be the best at whatever job I had. I wanted to be the first to do something. Even proximity to the best made me feel like the best. Unfortunately, this competitive streak also reared its head in motherhood. I wondered what being the best looked like in the mom world.

It was easy to research since Instagram was a popular place to display motherhood wins. I quickly began noticing what pictures got the most likes. What stellar moms seemed to be followed the most. Competition ensued, and the race began.

Nothing can reveal our need to be the best mom more than end-of-the-year activities in elementary school. There was no shortage of events and opportunities, and I felt like I had to do them all. In order to win, to be the best, no stone could be left unturned. The end of the school year looked like:

Last-minute presentations (FYI, this was not fun for
    anybody)
Recitals
Field trips
End-of-year honors programs
Parties and celebrations
Final tests and school projects

Why do we cram so much into one month?!

Even though there were eight million events that May, I still felt like I hadn't done enough. I tried to be present as much as possible, but social media reminded me I had not done a good job tracking our memories and celebrating the milestones (online, at least). My effort in competing for best mom had left me feeling tired both emotionally and physically. Between the last week of elementary school for Sinclair and trying to find a new home, I hadn't posted about the honors program for either of my daughters. I hadn't posted about the piano recital and the award won. I hadn't posted about all the celebrations. And it wasn't just that I hadn't posted—I hadn't even taken pictures to post. Which left me feeling like I'd earned the World's Most Average Mom Award. I definitely didn't take first place as Mom of the Year.

I have a feeling you know exactly how I felt. Even though raising kids has revealed that my competitive nature still exists, it has also forced me to grow up my view of winning. Winning in motherhood was labeled as thriving. Everywhere I turned, I was told to *thrive, to flourish, to prosper in raising kids*. Those moms I saw unmoved by the mess, desiring to be with their kids all the time or unfrazzled by tantrums looked like a perfect picture of thriving. Thriving felt like first place, and I felt like I kept finishing in last place because, so much of the time, I felt like I wasn't flourishing in this role or prospering in any shape or form.

If ever there was a time when parents should be given permission to lower the bar of parenting excellence, it's in the middle of a freaking pandemic. But you'd be surprised how many mothers are still competing for first place. Easter arrived just a month into the pandemic, and I thought for sure people would collectively decide that Easter baskets wouldn't happen this year. But when I looked at Instagram, I was surprised to see how many people still pulled them off. Kids were receiving all sorts of extravagant Easter baskets despite the quarantines in place.

We feel pressure to "thrive" in all we do. But to me, thriving felt like an impossible standard. As I wrestled with the word *thrive*, I realized I had a mixed view of it. To me, thriving meant achieving perfection, which in turn meant winning. The more I focused on thriving as I defined it, the more I felt like I was losing. That's when I started to think about what winning really looked like for me in motherhood. And I started to realize I was winning when I simply showed up.

Showing up when I felt tired was winning.

Showing up at any school event was winning.

Showing up at home while missing the school event was also winning.

Getting to the end of the day and choosing to show up again tomorrow was winning.

Being present was winning.

I may not have taken pictures of every experience, but I was present. And that is enough. I am learning that the best I can do today is to *show up* and *be present.* If you are looking for what makes you a good parent, a good wife, a good friend, a good person, that is the criteria. You show up. You are present. Being engaged is what counts.

That said, I still find myself competing at times—striving for the blue ribbon. This is especially true when the days are hard.

One day, around 6 p.m., I sent Scott a text that read, "Just FYI, everyone is on the crazy train today." I wanted to make sure he was mentally and emotionally prepared to walk into our home. Raising girls is no joke when it comes to emotions. And raising girls who have big emotions is even harder. My girls can go from zero to sixty instantly, and their emotions change with the wind.

Some days are hard from the beginning, and that day was a doozy from the start. Anxiety was running high. My daughter was receiving a series of anonymous text messages, and her anxiety was through the roof. Helping tweens navigate the art of carrying on a conversation face-to-face is hard enough, but helping them figure out how to dialogue via texting takes it to another level. Too much for my daughter. As she waited for the person to respond, I saw her anxiety building. I told her to do something with her anxiety, instead of staring at the screen waiting for words to appear. So she ran laps around our sofa, then pulled out the Trouble game and started hitting the plastic bubble over and over for at least a minute (which felt like an hour).

For once, I responded well. I said, "It sounds like you're trying to figure out what to do with your anxiety while you wait to hear back from whoever texted you. I understand the feeling, but I'm gonna need you to manage your anxiety in another way before my head explodes from that game."

We survived, and she went to school. Winning.

Then she came home after surviving an entire day with people and classes and circumstances out of her control. From there, things went downhill quickly. Objects were thrown. Words were shouted. Threats were made. I felt like someone needed to hand me a trophy because I kept my cool and responded in a calm voice during the entire saga, which lasted nearly two hours.

At the end of the night, I was spent. I felt like I had run a marathon both physically and emotionally.

When morning came, though, I showed up. Showing up may be the greatest act of love in parenting. When the dust settles after a fight, when you're streaked with sweat and tears, the best thing you can do is show up. You remind your kids that they are loved. And you show up because that's the most courageous thing you can do. Showing up is enough.

My older daughter spends most of her free time at the horse farm. Sinclair has always had a great affinity for horses. When she isn't riding, she's working at the farm—cleaning stalls, catching horses in the field, or bathing them.

One day, I arrived at the farm to pick her up, and as soon as she got in the car, she broke down in tears. Usually she's all smiles, but that day, the work was hard. She had to oil saddles for over two hours, and then she had to redo the job, which meant no time to ride. I think she was feeling a combination of exhaustion, disappointment, and embarrassment. Unmet expectations at any age can leave us in tears.

I normally don't handle big or negative emotions well, whether they are my own or someone else's. I like to breeze right on past them with quick fixes. And often I'm running at full speed between work obligations and family needs. I'm not typically in a place where I can sit still with emotions. But for once, I was in a restful, ready place, and I could meet my daughter's sadness with gentleness. Handling emotions isn't easy. It can be exhausting and is almost never convenient. But in that moment, Sinclair needed a safe place to land. A shelter from the storm. No solutions. Just compassion.

So she sat in the seat beside me and cried. I listened and offered my understanding and my presence. No fixes. When we arrived home, I sat with her while she ate a late dinner. Instead of homework, we played a few rounds of a card game.

As we said good night, I asked her the question I'd been asking each night: "What are you thankful for? What made you smile today?" Her usual answer involved a horse, but this time she thought about it for a minute. Then she looked at me and said, "You." It wasn't a trite answer. It wasn't a generic answer. I knew it was true. That night, I showed up. I listened. I engaged. I was present. And she noticed.

When we give our kids our presence, we are choosing to become a safe haven for them. Because here's what I know to be true: You can't multitask presence. You can't be thinking about your agenda while trying to comfort a child.

You can't prevent your children from feeling disappointed, sad, embarrassed, or exhausted, but you can be gentle, present, and safe. You can provide what you can provide. Presence looks like showing up, and it is enough.

There's a statement I find helpful to say out loud to myself: *You have permission to take yourself out of the running for being the best.* This statement really speaks to my competitive nature.

It reminds me not to measure my worth by how well I perform.

It reminds me that what matters most is being engaged and present.

It reminds me that winning doesn't always mean taking first place.

It reminds me that doing the best I can is enough.

It encourages me to do my best but not worry about being the best.

Letting go of the desire to be Supermom is still a struggle. But when I recognize the hustle happening, I remind myself that third place is just fine. Some days call for a lower standard of excellence.

Cereal for dinner. Fine.

Not the smartest in class. Fine.

Didn't come in first place. Fine.

Netflix all day. Fine.

We need to lower the bar of expectation. Be okay with being the world's most average mom if the race is about what others think of you. Be okay with being the world's most average mom if the race is based on meeting the sometimes unrealistic expectations of others. Because if you are present, you are more than an okay mom.

Let's stop striving to be the best. Let's instead choose to show up. We don't have to be the most awesome mom on the block.

Give yourself permission to take yourself out of the running. Showing up is brave. It takes courage to acknowledge where you are, to face the hard, and to choose to show up again and again.

It takes grit to face a hard day and show up again tomorrow.

It takes resolve to be present even if you don't take pictures.

It takes mettle to be engaged even if hearing about LEGOs bores you to tears.

It takes courage to show up. And showing up is enough.

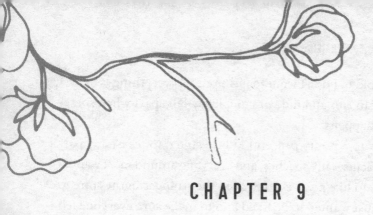

CHAPTER 9

I COULD BE WRONG

When it comes to all these things I'm writing about, I feel like I've gained more ground on some than on others. I've been working on things like being courageous and overcoming failure for years. I've been learning and practicing and growing for a long time. And yet sometimes I still feel like a baby deer first attempting to walk. I try to stand but my legs feel all wobbly. I'm trying to be better at some things but still feel like I've barely taken a baby step forward. Take, for example, the way I deal with conflict.

I've quickly realized that I'm going to *have* to figure out how to handle conflict because I have to teach these wild animals, I mean young humans, how to handle it. Our house can be full of conflict on any given day. And I can't teach what I don't know.

Before I say anything else, I must be honest. I am nearly forty-two years old and still figuring this out. For the love. Nonetheless, we're gonna talk about it because I want to be better at it. I don't want to avoid it. I don't want to just pretend everything is okay. I don't want to run and hide or completely fall apart when something bad happens.

I grew up a pretty peaceful kid. I wanted to please my parents, my teachers, my coaches, and everyone around me. I wanted my friends to like me. I even wanted the stranger in the store to like me. I just wanted to be liked and to make sure everyone felt a sense of peace. I didn't want to be a drama-inducing person or someone who rocked the boat.

My lack of experience in dealing with conflict goes way back. My brother is nearly four years older than me, so I grew up basically feeling like an only child. I didn't have knock-down-drag-outs with my brother. Sibling conflicts just didn't really exist (at least from what I can remember). He pretty much ignored my existence (like many older siblings do). Conflict successfully avoided.

The truth is, I never really learned how to deal with conflict. And because I wanted everyone to like me and everyone to get along, I avoided it altogether or resorted to passive-aggressive behavior. The thought of confronting someone was too much to consider.

But if there is one thing I know to be true about parenting, it's that you will deal with more conflict than you ever imagined. I remember when Jennifer Walker, one of the founders of Moms on Call, told me not to be concerned when newborn Sinclair cried. That crying was her only form of exercise at this age. But her crying always felt like an assault on my life. Her crying sounded like a pterodactyl coming to kill me.

And then when you add more kids to the picture, especially if they are close in age, conflict rises fast. It's no longer just a cute newborn crying for exercise; it's big kids exercising their right to be heard no matter the cost. On any given day, my girls wage war against each other for any number of reasons. They fight like a scene straight from *The Hunger Games*, especially if one dared take a certain LEGO from the other. They fight over the remote, where to sit on the sofa, who rides in the front seat of the car, who gets the last yogurt, and whether the sun is shining. You name it, they fight over it.

In fact, I remember one day when the fighting was off the charts. It had been constant, unceasing. Finally I looked at my girls and said, "If I die, please tell people it was because your fighting caused blood to pour from my ears until I died."

But we don't just experience conflict in our homes with our kids or between our kids. We experience conflict with our partners, our friends, our neighbors, our coworkers, and sometimes even the random people we encounter day to day. Conflict is inevitable. I used to think that if I pleased, perfected, and performed enough, conflict wouldn't happen. But I've learned that's just not how the world works.

Take the following incident. One night, Scott and I took a walk around the block after dinner. We walked for over twenty minutes, and I must have gone on and on about nothing. When we returned, the girls were occupied with crafts, so we took advantage of their preoccupation to sit outside and continue our conversation about nothing. Except Scott turned the conversation to something more than nothing. He talked about how he had an idea about what he wanted to do next for work.

Fast-forward twenty minutes, and conflict had entered the scene. It was stealthy. I didn't even know it had crept in until it was too late. Long story short, he felt like I didn't care about his thoughts and ideas. I sat there, deflated. I'd showed up and tried my best, but my best wasn't enough. Scott hadn't felt seen in that moment. I'd been present and engaged, but conflict still happened. It didn't involve screaming or fighting; it was more like our wires had gotten crossed, leaving us feeling disconnected.

Still, I'm learning a few things about how to handle conflict instead of avoiding it. First, I'm learning to get curious. I ask myself questions like, *What am I feeling? Have I done what this person has suggested I've done? What does this conflict cause me to believe about myself?* Instead of running away from the conflict in my head or listing out all the negative things about myself to confirm that I didn't please, perfect, or perform enough, by getting curious I'm able to see that conflict doesn't have to be a bad thing. The tension can cause good. The tension is necessary for me to learn and grow and develop.

As a part of getting curious about conflict, I've learned a phrase that I want my girls to know. I am learning to say, "I could be wrong." This is a hard phrase for me to say. Do you know what I don't like? Being wrong. It has always been that way for me. I love to be right, to be the fastest, to be the prettiest, to be the funniest. And this attitude works well if you have the right places to channel it. Growing up as an athlete, I found that this mindset worked great. That's the beauty of competition. But the problem came when this mentality bled into my relationships. I wanted to win the fight with Scott or make sure my kids knew I was right, and they were wrong. I wanted the last word.

The phrase, "I could be wrong" didn't really exist in my vocabulary until I had kids. Having kids is what highlighted my inability to handle conflict. I had always been able to rely on doing the right thing and trying to appear perfect. I was a peacemaker at heart, and my job was to make everyone happy and not rock the boat (while also making sure I was the best, of course).

But guess who rocks all the boats? Kids. They don't give a flying monkey about keeping the peace. The relationship between our kids was peaceful until Rory was old enough to decide she didn't want to go along with whatever Sinclair wanted to do. And that rocked the boat. Conflict ensued.

Because I usually thought conflict was a cue to step back rather than a cue to flex a muscle, I avoided it. But I've realized that the more I can approach others with the posture of *I could be wrong*, the more I come to value the relationship over being right.

Susan Clarke and CrisMarie Campbell were guests on *Surviving Sarah* to talk about conflict in relationships.[1] They illustrated how conflict isn't a bad thing but is instead something that can improve relationships. When we feel like we're right, we can still value the relationship. They recommended saying, "Right now, I feel right, and I'm stuck there." By speaking that honest truth, you are creating the possibility that you can move. That is valuing the relationship over being right.

The phrase, "I could be wrong," carries a certain sense of humility with it. Imagining a world where I could be wrong breaks down relationship barriers. The phrase enables us to lean in when conflict arises and relationships are strained, and to imagine a different ending. Our world is full of tension. (I'm looking at you, Twitter.) If there is anything we are passionate about or perceive as absolute truth, there is a good chance things will get heated when someone disagrees with us. That's because our focus is on being right. But imagine how different the world would be if we approached the topics we felt so passionately about with a sense of humility—where we valued the relationship over being right. Imagine starting any hard conversation from a place where your goal isn't to convince the other person that you are right but instead to admit that you could be wrong.

I believe this about parenting, but I could be wrong.

I believe this about the Bible, but I could be wrong.

I believe this about politics, but I could be wrong.

Valuing the relationship over being right looks like believing the best about someone. Before you jump to conclusions, you try to give them the most generous benefit of the doubt. This type of generosity helps guard us against unmerited judgment.

Being generous with our thoughts and hearts toward others looks like choosing to believe the best. So much can go wrong in relationships—words and actions can be misinterpreted or misunderstood so easily, especially with social media comments or texting, where you can't read someone's tone or facial expressions. Elevating the relationship means choosing to believe the best. You have to believe this person *loves* you and is *for* you—unless you hear otherwise.

One of the tools that helped me start believing the best about others is the phrase, "The story I'm telling myself . . ." In Brené Brown's book *Rising Strong*, Brené talks about how we look to make sense of things that don't make sense.[2] So we make up stories in our heads.

Once, when one of my friends had distanced herself from me, I reached out to her with a text that read, "The story I'm telling myself about why you are avoiding me is that I have hurt you. And I would like the opportunity to talk about it and apologize if that story is true."

I laid down my former method of avoidance or passive-aggressiveness and chose to be *for* the relationship. It didn't solve the tension in the relationship, but it was most certainly a step in the right direction toward learning how to choose the relationship over being right.

What would it look like if you chose to see conflict as a good tension that can build up relationships instead of viewing it as something to avoid? I can see the potential. But even as I write, my ears are still bleeding from the screaming taking place outside my room. Someone took the last Reese's cup. We may not make it out alive. But I will choose to keep working on myself—to value conflict instead of running away from it. I will keep learning alongside my girls to admit my part of the conflict and take ownership where needed. I will keep stepping forward with the posture that I could be wrong. I will strive to believe the best about others and be generous with my thoughts toward them. And I will elevate the relationship over my need to be right.

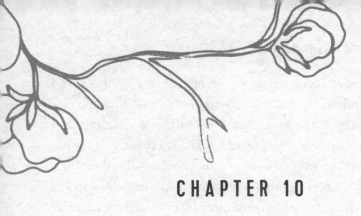

CHAPTER 10

I'M SORRY

Have you ever done something you totally regretted? Maybe you've experienced buyer's remorse. When you were standing in the aisle at Target, purchasing yet another item designed by America's sweetheart, Joanna Gaines, seemed like a good idea. But when you got home, you wished you hadn't purchased it. Or maybe it was buyer's remorse over something bigger. My husband has had buyer's remorse over almost every home we've purchased.

Maybe you regretted something you ate. You know you should stay away from dairy, but that pizza was just too appetizing, and you paid for it later.

Maybe you said something online you know you really shouldn't have said. You knew trolling this person would only bring out the worst in you, yet you did it anyway. And after some liquid courage in the form of red wine, you decided it made perfect sense to comment. (No, just me?) Immediate regret.

I remember being newly pregnant with my firstborn and taking a family vacation. My niece was only three. I had no clue about toddlers. I had never heard about the terrible threes. I didn't know there was such a thing. I was just a sweet, bright-eyed twentysomething who was completely oblivious about motherhood. After witnessing my niece's countless meltdowns in the face of life-threatening circumstances like not getting an extra Oreo, I looked at Scott and said, "I think we made the wrong choice. It's too late to turn back, but I think deciding to have kids was a mistake." Bless my heart.

Regret comes in all shapes and sizes, and none of us are immune to it.

For some of us, raising kids can bring its own set of regrets. Some are small, some are big. Some of us regret our choice of feeding—bottle or breast. Some of us regret how we handled vaccinations or what schools we sent our kids to. When you set out on your parenting journey, nobody tells you that you will make mistakes and trip up more times than you can imagine. Most of us assumed that if we read all the books, listened to everyone's stories and advice, and prayed enough, we would bypass all the regrets we'd heard from others. We thought we'd be different.

But we aren't.

At this point in my parenting journey, I'm learning to give myself a lot of grace as I look back. However, it's not always easy to look your regrets in the face.

One thing I regret is how I handled discipline. Again, I had no idea what I was doing. When Sinclair was six months old, I'd already placed a rush Amazon order for books about discipline. I was convinced that if I just read all the books, I could figure it out—you know, A + B = C. But at that point I had a baby who only slept, ate, and cooed, so reading discipline books didn't really translate.

Looking back, I can see that I was living in a vacuum. I had surrounded myself with like-minded people, which was good in so many ways, but if we never allow ourselves to befriend people who are different from us, we'll miss out on different perspectives and different ways of doing things. We start to believe there is only one way to do something, and this thinking is especially dangerous when it comes to raising kids. We start to live a binary life—this or that, black or white, right or wrong.

Because of the vacuum I lived in, I thought a harsh discipline style was needed. I thought I had to be an enforcer of the rules. An enforcer of what was right and wrong. I based my reasoning largely on my interpretation of a certain passage of the Bible: "Those who spare the rod of discipline hate their children. Those who love their children care enough to discipline them" (Prov. 13:24).

Basically, spare the rod, spoil the child. Enforcer needed. So I put on my cop uniform and set out to keep watch over my kids' behavior. As a strong competitor, I wasn't going to let anything get past me. They weren't gonna pull a fast one on me. Not on my watch!

I couldn't leave any stone unturned. If I didn't address their behavior and, more specifically, what was going on in their hearts, my children's futures would be in jeopardy. I stressed about learning Bible verses that addressed wrong behaviors because I felt so much pressure to make sure they knew they were sinners who were disobeying God. I needed to make sure they made that connection—even at the early age of two. Their souls were at stake.

I remember preschool Sinclair trying to connect the dots of

how she had sinned against God by throwing her cup at her sister. I tried to talk to her about her anger problem and what that said about her heart. Not surprisingly, she didn't get it. She looked so confused when I told her that not only did she need to apologize to her sister, but she also needed to apologize to God. I did nothing but bewilder her when I tried to explain that she had somehow offended this invisible divine being whom even adults don't fully understand.

Regret.

My harsh style of discipline did nothing good for my heart or my children's. Most of the time, spanking felt good because I was working out my own frustration. You may think I typed that easily, but it's not easy to be vulnerable in this way. At the time, spanking honestly felt like the easiest way to deal with misbehavior. I was the enforcer.

Regret.

All I was accomplishing, though, was positioning myself *against* my child, not *for* my child. When I eventually made that discovery, regret flooded my heart. How could I have been so cruel? How could I have thought my children's intentions were evil? My misguided approach had made me believe their natural makeup was flawed. It pushed me to see their wrongness instead of their uniqueness.

Your child might be hard to parent because she bumps up against all the boundaries. But maybe that says more about her personality than the state of her heart. Maybe she will be strong enough to stand up for herself one day. I thought my daughter was supposed to respect and obey me at all times, so instead of seeing the traits of her personality, I saw her as bad. I positioned myself against her, not for her.

Regret.

I didn't believe positivity would work. It felt like I was letting my child off the hook. But when I stepped back and looked at myself, things started to change. How do I like to be treated? What works well with me when I've messed up? I know for sure that the bad cop, the enforcer, doesn't work for me. Yet somehow I thought it would work for my daughters.

I started to understand this idea better when we got our dog, Murray. Now, speaking of regrets, we fondly refer to Murray as the greatest regret of 2017. Let me paint the scene. Sinclair was nine and Rory was seven. We had a beloved cat, Tippy, who had been with us since our first year of marriage. Now, Tippy was an amazing cat, but like most cats, he chose whom he loved. He loved Rory, but Sinclair? Not so much. Rory was gentle with him and Sinclair wanted to play rough, which meant he often snubbed her. Consequently, I *knew* we needed a dog. We needed a pet who would love unconditionally, who wouldn't mind rough play.

So I started looking for dogs. We couldn't afford a fancy pure-bred, so I took to the local rescue shelters. But being approved to be a pet owner was intense. After filling out extensive paperwork and conducting a phone interview, I was told by the adoption facilitator that finding a dog for our family would be difficult because we were classified as "high risk." *I'm sorry, what?* Since we had a cat and two kids, we were high risk. *I'm sorry, don't most people get dogs for their kids?* The adoption facilitator would need to make a home visit to determine if we could be approved. If you've gotten to know me at all, what happened next shouldn't surprise you. I hung up the phone. I'm out. When I was a kid, dogs just showed up at our door. Literally. "Mom, there's a sad dog looking in the window. Can we keep it?" We didn't go to a rescue shelter. We rescued these dogs ourselves.

That's when I decided to bring Jesus into the situation. I asked Jesus to just send us a dog. And would you believe it, the very next day my friend Merica announced on Instagram that she'd found a puppy in a pizza box by her house. I immediately knew that was our answer. I mean, I had *just* asked for a dog. Ask and you shall receive. Right?

Murray is adorable, but he's ninety-five pounds and all paws. He loves to track mud into the house and clobber everyone who enters with his legs and kisses.

Regret.

But having Murray has taught me about parenting with positivity versus parenting as the enforcer. For the first couple of years with him, I was perpetually frustrated. He was unruly and couldn't obey to save his life. I would constantly say, "Bad dog!" I treated him the exact same way I had tried to parent my kids. But at some point, something shifted in me. I started speaking to Murray based not on how he was behaving but on how I wanted him to behave. If I wanted him to come inside, I would say, "Come, Murray! What a good dog!" I would say that over and over until he came in. *What a good dog!* I've done this so much that he does whatever I ask of him whenever he hears the phrase, "Good dog." I started using this positive phrase all the time, saying, "Good dog!" as I rubbed him under his chin. This approach worked so well with Murray that I decided to try it out with Sinclair.

One day as I rubbed Murray's chin and said, "Good dog," I saw Sinclair standing beside us, smiling. So I turned to her and said, "What if I treated you the way I treat Murray?" She giggled. I looked her in the eyes and started tickling her under the chin, saying, "Such a good girl!" over and over. That girl lit up like the sky on the Fourth of July. I spoke over her what her heart had been longing to hear. She carries enough shame without any extra being piled on her. She knows when she's done something wrong. It was time she heard some positivity from the one she looks up to the most.

Good girl.

If I'm being honest, that's exactly what works with me. If you want me to change something, work on something, iron out something, approaching me in a way that speaks good over who I am works far better than negativity.

I want to be *for* my kids, not *against* them.

Some of the best conversations with my girls happen in the car or on walks. Being in motion seems to be a catalyst for vulnerability. One day as I drove in the car with eleven-year-old Sinclair, I told her that sometimes I don't get things right in parenting—and that she experiences most of my mistakes because she's the first. I sometimes do things I regret—things I later wish I'd done differently. I told her that I wish I'd never spanked her. I said, "I'm sorry I spanked you. Did you feel loved when I spanked you?" She thought for a minute, then shook her head no. "I'm sorry for doing something that made you question my love for you," I told her.

Something powerful happens when we utter those two little words: *I'm sorry.* I don't like saying those words. I don't like realizing I messed up. I try to avoid hurting people at all costs. But parenting has taught me how much those words are needed. When we're the enforcer, it's easy to believe that we have to have it all together and that if we mess up, we should sweep it under the rug. But I want my girls to learn how to apologize. I want them to be able to own their part in something. When kids develop this ability, empathy follows.

And it all starts with me.

By no means do I have the perfect approach to discipline. My girls still drive me up the wall. They still push all my buttons. I still want to pull out that enforcer badge. I still struggle to say, "I'm sorry." But I'm working on laying down the badge and instead picking up my cheerleader pom-poms.

Imagine what it would look like if you started speaking to your kids the way you want to be spoken to. What would the temperature in your home begin to feel like? What if you started modeling for your kids how to take ownership of your regrets or mistakes? Maybe the space between you will diminish.

Life is more than binary. It's complicated and seldom boils down to black and white or right and wrong. "I'm sorry" is a powerful phrase—a phrase that can build connection. Life will always include some regrets. We can't prevent them, but we can strengthen our connection to those we love with those two little words "I'm sorry."

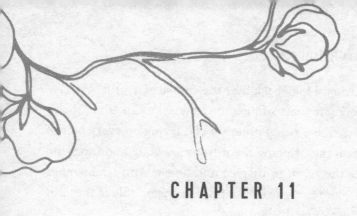

CHAPTER 11

TAKE A SMOKE BREAK

Do you ever feel like you have a certain theme to your parenting? Like maybe there's a lesson that smacks you in the face time and time again? Or maybe there's just a certain rub that continues no matter how many times you've tried to figure out a way around it? I've been parenting for twelve years now, and not only have I yet to figure out how to manage my own emotions, but I'm also still trying to figure out how to help a not-yet-developed kid learn to manage her emotions.

My kids can go from tranquil to turbulent instantly. One minute they're fine and the next their world is burning down. Eyes roll. Doors slam. "I hate you's" are screamed. Objects are thrown. And I am left standing completely dumbfounded about what to do next.

Can somebody please give me a surefire strategy for helping my girls manage their own emotions?

I never would have described myself as a highly emotional

person, yet when I look back over the course of my life, I've certainly had my fair share of meltdowns (even as an adult). I can distinctly remember being nineteen and trying on every pair of jeans I owned, then ripping them from my body and throwing them across the room in disgust and anger. And I remember stepping barefoot in a pile of dog poop in the middle of the yard and erupting in anger instantly.

Some of my most intense meltdowns have happened while trying to parent. Nothing pushes me further, faster, than a child who knows how to push all my buttons. A couple of months ago, while in the beginning stages of quarantine due to COVID-19, I had one of my biggest breakdowns to date. I can't remember how this explosion was ignited, but two parties participated: me and my older daughter. I'm sure our emotions were already on edge because life had been turned upside down, and I was now trying to work and write a book from home while also attempting to homeschool my girls—all while facing the uncertainty of whether we would have enough food or toilet paper to survive another week.

I wish I could say this was a one-time instance, but I can recall several epic meltdowns over the years that weren't induced by living in quarantine. I can remember losing my mind over potty training, sassy mouths, and standoffs over bedtime.

For so long, I thought I had to avoid feeling the negative emotions—mad, sad, frustrated, discouraged. Maybe if I'd done enough self-care before I reached my pushed-too-far point, I wouldn't have felt those feelings. And while that may be true to a certain degree—maybe I could have headed off the outburst if I'd taken better care of myself—feeling negative emotions isn't bad or wrong. It's human. I've learned that when I feel those feelings,

I need to pay attention. And paying attention looks like asking questions. *Why am I feeling this way? Why are my girls exploding? Why are they feeling this way?* And then, *What can I do to get my brain back to a thinking brain?*

I've had so many conversations with my dear friends Sissy Goff and David Thomas about this very thing. They explain that in those moments when we feel out of control, the oxygen moves from the front of the brain to the back, and in order to think clearly, we have to get the oxygen back to the front. Something physiological is happening. In their amazing book *Are My Kids on Track?* they say, "It makes no sense to engage with kids with discipline or correction when they are experiencing elevated emotions. The brain is flooded. No person (child or adult) is capable of having perspective in those moments. We can't think rationally. We're incapable of being our best selves."[1] Science accounts for why we can't think straight when our emotions are skyrocketing. Everything in our bodies is connected—and our bodies are trying to tell us something.

In those instances when either we're about to explode or we've already done so, we need to do something to get our brain back. Do you know what helps? Breathing. Yup, something that simple. I've learned that I'm more of a hold-your-breath kind of girl. Guess who else is that way? My older daughter. In fact, when she was an infant, she would get so angry that she would scream at the top of her lungs while holding her breath until she passed out. No kidding—she would scream and then all of a sudden the noise would stop because she passed out from holding her breath. Talk about scary for a new mom (and for every nursery worker she came into contact with)!

When we hold our breath, we refuse to allow oxygen to get

to our brain. That's science, friends. And we need the oxygen to return so that we can think clearly.

Let's go back to that meltdown I mentioned earlier. Here I was in the middle of a meltdown, holding my breath and wondering why I couldn't calm down. I had to start thinking about how to get myself to breathe, to take a break from the crazy of the moment. That's when it hit me.

I needed a smoke break.

Not literally. I've never smoked a cigarette in my life, but it dawned on me one day that people who smoke often get to stop what they are doing, walk outside, and take a break. As they smoke, they breathe in and exhale out. That is exactly what we need to do: stop what we're doing, walk away, and breathe.

As easy as this sounds, it's not. It's not easy for me to walk away from a fight or an opportunity to make sure the other party knows I'm right. And it's not easy if you have a kid who, as you try to walk away from the crazy, follows you. Walking away feels like giving in, but it also feels like a cop-out. Like you are abandoning the issue or the person. Many of us were taught to come to a resolution right away—don't let the sun go down on your anger. So we push through with our emotions on high. But what we really need to do is step away and figure out how to breathe.

Recently, my daughter started yelling at me for something related to school that was somehow my fault, and I. just. lost it. I'm talking code-red, sound-the-alarm kind of losing it. I felt anger rising in me like hot lava. As I yelled at the top of my lungs, I realized I was about to completely cuss my daughter out. And in that moment, I stopped, turned on a dime, grabbed my earbuds, and went outside for a walk (aka Mama's taking a smoke break).

And as I walked, I listened to music so loudly that I felt like I was in a vacuum. I even yelled out as I walked. I had to get it all out. I walked for nearly an hour that day—I needed longer than five minutes to calm down. With each step, I took a breath. I knew I had to get my brain to return to thinking rationally and soundly. Once I was calm, I returned to the house. My daughter had been given space to calm down as well since her antagonizer had left the house. And we were able to address what was going on in a more reasonable way.

We *have* to start taking smoke breaks. Feeling negative emotions isn't bad, but allowing them to damage your relationship with someone is. It is normal to be upset, pushed, or strained at times, but when you feel that way, pay attention and take a break.

A few years ago, my girls and I went to an occupational therapist for six months. She helped us learn how to manage our emotions. We learned many techniques from our therapist, but one thing that really stuck was using language to describe what we're feeling. She described how our insides are like an engine, and that engine can run high, low, or just right. So when one of us was feeling on the brink of exploding, we could say, "My engine is running really high," signaling that we need to do something to help it come back down to just right.

In the car the other day, my daughter's engine was running really high because of some friend drama. After some time, I could feel my own engine revving up. She was freaking out about everything by this point—the trucks driving beside us were too close, her sister was looking at her funny, and the sun wasn't shining bright enough. I found myself about to have a full-on breakdown. So I said (really, it was sort of a yell), "My engine is running really high, and I need time and space for it to come back down. Since we're stuck in the car, I need you to stop talking." Then I put on my favorite Spotify playlist and no one spoke for the next twenty minutes. That's what I needed. That was my smoke break. We need to take them where we can get them.

What can we do in the moment to help us manage our emotions? What does a smoke break in the middle of the crisis look like for you?

Here are some ideas:

- Go for a walk.
- Take deep breaths in and out slowly for one minute.
- Scream into a pillow.
- Go outside and scream (my mom used to go down to the creek on our property to scream and throw rocks).
- Punch a pillow.
- Write down all the things you want to say (and maybe throw away the list later).
- Do something physical like a HIIT workout.
- Lock yourself in your room.
- Read something.
- Draw something.
- Take a shower or simply sit in the bathroom and run the water.
- Listen to music.
- Dance it out.
- Go for a drive.
- Journal.
- Call a friend.

You don't need to feel pressured to remain in the situation or fix everything in that moment. Remove yourself. Take a break. Give yourself the time and space to rein in your emotions.

But we also need to take care of ourselves *before* the crisis hits. The more we can take care of our engine before it revs up, the less on edge we will be. I find that when I have time to myself and opportunities to do the things that help me function better, I am less likely to have a full-on explosion. Many people call this *self-care*—doing something that cares for your own needs.

I want to challenge you to do something . . .

Daily. Think about what you enjoy doing that doesn't cost you anything. Maybe it's drinking a cup of coffee in the morning all by yourself. Or having your favorite drink on the patio at night under the twinkle lights. Or taking fifteen minutes to sit outside and soak up the sun. Or going for a walk on a local trail or greenway. It's important to do something every day that refreshes you. For me, I drink my first cup of coffee *alone*. It allows me to have space to think before I interact with anyone else. I made a rule that my girls can't come out of their room before 7:30 a.m. (And if they dare exit their rooms earlier, they receive a strong stink eye and a swift finger pointing them back to their rooms.)

Weekly. Think about what you enjoy doing that doesn't cost much. Maybe enlist the help of your spouse or a friend or sitter for an hour or two. Maybe you could go to Target alone or to Starbucks. You'd be surprised how much refreshment a $5 outing to Starbucks can bring. I treat myself to Starbucks once a week. (Clearly, I have a love affair with coffee.) I sit there alone or sometimes with a friend, but taking a small amount of time away from the kids breathes life back into my weary soul.

Monthly. Think about what you enjoy doing that costs a

little more time and money. Maybe it's going to your favorite restaurant. Or booking a hotel for a night or scheduling a spa treatment. For Scott and me, date night doesn't happen weekly but monthly. Having that time on the calendar gives me something to look forward to. And I always come back home feeling rejuvenated.

Not only is taking care of yourself good for your emotional, relational, and spiritual well-being, but it's good for your kids to see you care for yourself. Some of the best advice I received when I was single was to guard my time off. My boss said, "Take care of yourself. No matter how busy you are, you must rest. Because if you don't do it now while you have a freer schedule, it will be even harder to start when you have kids."

Recognize, too, that you and your spouse aren't the only busy people in your family. Your kids are busier than you were at their age. Model to them what it means to take care of yourself. Let them see you relax. Let them see you enjoy refreshment. Let them see you and your spouse prioritize time away with each other so that they too will learn to find ways to renew their bodies, minds, and spirits.

Taking a smoke break is now a common theme in my parenting. In fact, my girls know I carry candy cigarettes in my purse. They think it's funny. But truly, I love that I can take something tangible like a smoke break to help them learn to manage their own emotions. If I want them to be able to manage their emotions effectively, I have to be able to manage my own.

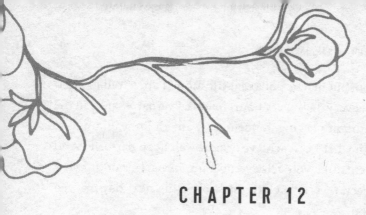

CHAPTER 12

NOTICE THE GOOD

When I was a little girl, I played with dolls all the time. My favorite doll was named Steve (I named him after one of my baby cousins). My mom even let me buy real baby stuff for my Steve—bottles, pacifiers, diapers. I had a blast dressing him up, feeding him, and rocking him to sleep. I loved pretending to be a mom.

Fast-forward twenty years to when I was handed my own real, live baby. This baby was much different from Steve. She wouldn't stop crying. Actually, let me be clear. Crying doesn't quite describe the sound she made. The noise was more like a pterodactyl's screech—and it just never stopped. She refused to take a bottle. She fought me when I tried to hold her a certain way to nurse. She refused to simply relax. It was like she existed at the highest terror threat level, alert just in case I decided to do something horrific like take a shower.

It didn't take long for me to realize that I was cut out to be a pretend mom but maybe not a real-life mom. I am wired to avoid conflict, yet every day (every hour) involved verbal assaults in the form of an infant's crying. Remember, I am an Enneagram 3—I find value in what I can achieve or how well I can perform. And often, it seems like you achieve nothing in parenthood. Every box you check reverts back to unchecked the next day or even the next hour.

Get them to sleep. Check. But then they wake up again.

Feed them. Check. But then they resume their crying.

Tell them not to throw blocks at me. Check. But they keep right on doing it.

Do the laundry. Check. But the hamper is full of dirty clothes again the next morning.

Every day was the same. Same routine. Same struggles. Never actually accomplishing anything.

I kept waiting for things to get better. Let me rephrase that. I kept waiting for my daughter to get better. Surely this wasn't about me! Maybe she will be different at age four. When that didn't happen, I thought maybe age five, when she started kindergarten. Then when that didn't happen, I thought maybe age ten. Well, news flash: things haven't changed. She is still her, and I am still me. Our personalities haven't changed. Most days still feel like two steps forward, one step back. (That has nothing to do with either of us being wrong. It's just because we are normal human beings.)

Is there any hope of surviving motherhood?

Somewhere along the way, I realized I had to stop expecting either of us to change. I know that may not be a surprising revelation to you, but it was to me. I wanted my *problem* to be solved. I wanted to check it off the list. I wanted things to be easy. I was trained to believe that if it's not easy, maybe you're not supposed to do it. And if your situation doesn't resolve, maybe you're supposed to quit and move on.

But you can't quit motherhood.

Don't we wish that raising kids was like using the Waze app? When we hit traffic, we're rerouted, or we can simply punch in a new destination. But that's not the case with motherhood. We can't just change our destination. The end goal is still to raise a child who is kind, capable, respectful, and responsible.

So if I can't quit and I can't change destinations, but I don't feel like my current approach is working, what can I do?

I've had the opportunity to interview quite a few experts on the podcast, including America's Supernanny, Dr. Deborah Tillman. Once while we were talking offline about some of the hard things I was facing in parenting, she advised me to change my posture toward my child and start noticing the good. She recommended I begin writing down all the good I see in my child.

Loyal, brave, caring, funny, strong.

I hate to admit this, but it was difficult to make the list. I had spent so much time compiling a list in my head of all the hard and negative things, no wonder my posture toward my daughters was defensive. Yet something powerful happens when we change the way we think. When we change the way we think, we change our lives.

Dr. Tillman also taught me how to reframe negative traits as positive ones. Instead of seeing my daughter's strong-willed nature as bad, I can see it as good. She has a fight in her that, when turned in the right direction, is a positive thing. Likewise, a messy room or cluttered brain can be seen as a sign of creativity.

Or someone who gets distracted easily may have a gift for noticing things and people.

Notice the good.

I started putting that phrase into practice and it helped change my perspective, not my destination, in parenting. Changing the way I think, intentionally noticing the good, has become one of my biggest survival skills in parenting.

When you feel unqualified . . .

When you feel like you just can't . . .

When you feel tired and the thought of another day of the same thing is too much . . .

When you feel like you just want to quit . . .

When you feel like you will never relate to a child who's different than you . . .

When you feel like you're going to crumble under the strength of a strong-willed kid . . .

I want you to notice the good.

That advice sounds easier than it actually is. Even today, as I write this, I struggle to notice the good. Dealing with preteen emotions is a whole new level of warfare that I never anticipated. It checks reason at the door. It fights for blood. And it fights what it perceives as injustice like anti-hunger activists fight the injustice of world hunger. The intensity is off the charts.

I want you to know that while my girl fights at home with tenacity, at school she is the picture of calm. Never gets in trouble. Isn't outspoken. Doesn't rock the boat. And because she's more reserved at school, she would often find herself picked on by one girl in particular. But my daughter would never fight back. She refused to stick up for herself.

One day in the car on the way to school, my girl waged an

attack against me. I'm sure I forgot to pack a snack or simply suggested that she brush her teeth—I know, I should be charged with war crimes for such things. I can't remember exactly why there was a fight, but I do remember telling her that this fight inside her was good. And if she would use that fight *for* good and to fight *for* herself or to fight *for* others, she would be unstoppable.

What difference would it make if this fire, this passion, this fight was reframed in my mind (and hers) as *good*? How would my attitude toward my daughter change if I was able to see the good in her tenacity? What shift would take place in my daughter if she could see all her qualities as good?

Fast-forward a few years. We were sitting around a table at the American Girl Café with some of her friends to celebrate her tenth birthday. One of the table cards asked the question: *Have you ever stood up to a bully?* My daughter's friends unanimously said, "Sinclair, you are great at standing up to bullies." I did a complete double take. *Wait, what?* My heart jumped out of my chest! Because there it was. The fight. Fighting *for* what was just and right. Fighting *for* others. Fighting *for* herself.

Notice the good.

Let me give you another example. Both of my girls are very chatty. There is no shortage of words. And when they started talking as little girls, I could never find a moment of silence (and still can't). I often feel like my ears are bleeding from all the words. I can remember one of my girls around the age of four having a desire to talk to everyone about everything. At every drive-through she'd say, "Roll down my window." Then, as the barista handed me my glory in a cup, my daughter would ask questions:

What's your name?

How's your day?

Are you married?

What's their name?

What job do they have?

No kidding, every drive-through. Every time.

It was cute the first time, but then I started to get irritated. Did she really have to talk to *everybody*? But I made myself notice the good. She was relational. She truly wanted to know people. She wanted them to feel known. I'm relational too, but in a different way. I tend to move quickly from one person to the next. The StrengthsFinder test would call me a WOO (Wins Others Over). I want people to feel seen, but I often don't allow time to let them feel known. But my girl wasn't interested in moving through a crowd quickly. She wanted people to know that they were really seen, really heard. What a great quality to have!

Notice the good.

As most parents know, bedtime can be one of the most frustrating and exhausting final battles of the day. Every parent is tired, yet somehow the kids always seem to find some unused energy. Many nights I find myself struggling to be loving, engaging, and present as I say good night. But do you know what happens every single night when I put Rory to bed, no matter how hard the day has been? Every night since she was four years old, she has spoken a benediction over me. She begins with ten kisses and ten hugs and then says, "I love you every morning. I love you every night. You're the best mom in the entire world. You are so sweet, sweet and kind to one another [not sure what she means by that, but I'm here for it]. And I hope you have sweet dreams."

What a little encourager she is! She will even say it if she's still struggling to get over something I did that she didn't like.

Notice the good.

What is it about your child that drives you insane? What is it that just rubs you the wrong way? Sometimes the answer to that question is the opposite of who you are. You are tidy. They are not. You prefer quiet. They do not. They love doing everything together. You don't.

What if you decided to push past the fact that parenting isn't easy and that you might not be qualified for this role and just decided to notice the good? What change would that make in your relationship with your children?

Okay, let me turn the tables now. As moms we probably find it easy to focus on how to better love and care for our kids, but in doing so we sometimes neglect to love and care for ourselves.

I think one of the reasons I have such a hard time noticing the good in my children is because I have a hard time noticing the good in myself. Often, I see a reflection of myself in my kids. And it's not usually a reflection I like. I see the things that annoy me about myself. I see the things I want to change in myself. I remember when I was a child and someone scolded me for being loud. Now, I wasn't really a particularly loud child, so more than likely this incident was the result of being a kid playing with other kids. As you know, put any number of kids together and the volume rises off the charts. Nonetheless, I remember that moment. It shaped me. I still have a hard time if someone asks me to be quiet or to speak more softly. But there's good in having a voice that carries. I'm a communicator for a living. I use my voice to speak on a daily basis. And just like with my children, I have to train myself to see the good in myself.

I feel things. I may not cry a lot, but I can definitely live emotionally in my head. I worry about what people think. I sometimes become someone I'm not in order to fit in. I can struggle with my appearance and with my relationship with food. I tend to focus on correcting things in my kids that I hate seeing in myself. But if I'm honest, I'm *overcorrecting* because I simply don't like those things about myself—I refuse to notice the good in myself.

When you find yourself overcorrecting something in your child or when you feel a sense of shame creep up on you when you watch your child say or do something that you recognize in yourself, take notice. Choose to notice the good. Silencing your inner critic will help you not to criticize your child. Moreover, when you start to notice the good in yourself, you'll be more apt to notice the good in others.

What if, every day, you chose to notice one good thing in your child—and in yourself? Ask yourself, "What is one thing that has been hard but that I can see the good in—both in myself and in my kids?"

Start there.

Then do it again tomorrow.

And the next day.

Notice the good. Pay attention and be curious. Life becomes more enjoyable and more abundant when we notice the good in ourselves and in our kids.

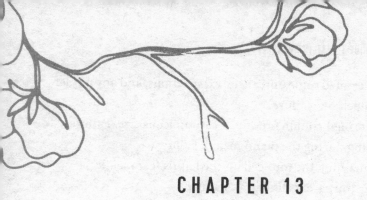

CHAPTER 13

BE KIND TO YOURSELF

While I am entirely thankful that raising my children is also raising me, acknowledging all the ways I need to grow is not always enjoyable. There are so many things that I had no idea needed improvement until I heard familiar words and saw familiar actions coming from my own girls. Where did they learn that? Oh, right—me!

For instance, I've never been one to handle mistakes well. I can trace this all the way back to my childhood. Somewhere along the way, I learned how to be a good girl. I learned how to please my parents, my teachers, my coaches, my peers. But with all that pleasing came a lot of pressure I put on myself to be right and to do right—especially the first time. I didn't like the reactions I got from people when I messed up. I didn't like how I felt when I disappointed people.

I became so good at *being* good that perfection became the

standard. I created some unrealistic expectations, and any unmet expectation felt like failure.

Discovering I couldn't fit into a certain jeans size. Failure.

Fumbling during the piano recital. Failure.

Not remaining the top seed on the tennis team. Failure.

Making my parents unhappy. Failure.

A boss telling me I could improve in a certain area. Failure.

Not getting the job. Failure.

Do you feel me?

I hear all the time about how good sports are for children because they help them learn about failure and loss. Playing sports supposedly teaches resiliency and determination. However, I was so hyperfocused on winning—doing it right, being perfect—that I didn't learn those valuable lessons when I lost a match or didn't make the team. Instead, I felt crushed. I felt like a failure.

Somewhere along the line, I started to equate love with performance. I started to believe that if I didn't perform well, if I made mistakes, if I failed, then I wouldn't be loved. Failure felt too vulnerable. It felt like showing up naked for all the world to see.

So I controlled everything.

I controlled what I ate so I could fit into those jeans.

I controlled how much I worked out so I could be the best on the tennis court.

I controlled how many hours I was willing to work so I could be the most productive at my job.

I controlled what I said and did in front of everyone so I could make everyone (except myself) happy.

I pleased people and perfected my life until I was completely exhausted. And naturally, this performance-based lifestyle carried over into raising kids.

We tend to develop our identity based on our behavior. That's true for your life and for your child's life. If we have gold-star behavior, we believe that we have a good identity—that we're good. And when we mess up or fail, we believe those experiences define our identity, too. We hear statements from our kids and in our own heads like "I'm a failure," "I'm a screw-up," "I'm unlovable." These are identity statements. They have nothing to do with behavior but everything to do with identity. *I am.* These are statements we would never say to someone we love, yet we don't hesitate to say them to ourselves. And our kids don't hesitate to say them to themselves.

I gained weight. I am fat.

I lied to my parents. I am a liar.

I burned dinner. I am a failure.

In the phase of adolescence my girls are currently in, kids tend to think about themselves and their identity a lot. And nothing shapes their identity more than their appearance and their performance. They believe that how they perform determines their identity. (Gosh, have I not graduated out of a tween's way of thinking?) I've always thought there is a lot of similarity between adolescents and adults. We, too, feel like our identity is shaped by our appearance and performance. Teenagers perform for parents, teachers, college admissions officers, coaches, peers, and social media contacts. Adults perform for parents, friends, our kids' teachers and coaches, strangers on the internet, and employers. And when a performance falls flat or downright fails, self-abasement tends to follow.

That has been true for the little girls I'm raising, but it has been true for this grown-up girl as well.

I would get upset when the baby cried. When she threw her

food on the floor. When she accidentally (or even purposefully) spilled something or made a mess. I would get so annoyed, frustrated, and angry. I was unaware of the impact of my reaction on them. I reacted to them the way I had always reacted to myself. Harshly.

Then I saw them begin to react to themselves in the same way. Seeing this familiar behavior in my kids helped me hear the critic in my own head. When one of my girls had trouble working a puzzle, or broke something, or spilled juice all over the floor, she would erupt with frustration. I would hear her scream, "I'm the worst kid in the world!" My girls reacted to their mistakes the same way their mama reacted to her own mistakes. It was like looking in a mirror.

Talk about breaking your heart. Hearing your child speak negatively about herself is painful. You know it isn't true, but trying to help her believe otherwise about herself is hard.

I knew I didn't want my girls to treat themselves with such meanness. I knew I wanted them to see that mistakes don't define who they are and don't have to lead to disconnection from others. And I knew this would have to start with me.

And so I started learning a new way to speak to myself. I realized that what I was saying to myself—and what I was hearing my girls say to themselves—was not the same thing I would say to a friend. I would never berate a friend for eating too many cookies, spilling the juice, or being unable to complete her work. I would speak with compassion. I would tell her, "That's okay."

I have a tendency to beat myself up for what I eat or drink. It's a long battle that I started fighting when I was a tween. And even now, as a fortysomething, I still beat myself up about it. Usually that voice is loudest in the middle of the night. I'll lie awake deriding myself for having had two glasses of wine or eating a handful of chips at 10 p.m. while watching TV. I'll think, *Why did you eat that? See, that's why your stomach isn't flat.* And I'll think on it as if I were on a one-loop roller coaster. Around and around I'll go. In my mind, mistakes like that aren't acceptable.

The first time my friend Sissy Goff joined me on the podcast, I misspelled her last name on the promotion material. Instead of Sissy Goff, I wrote Sissy *Golf*. Yup. Not the end of the world, but you would have thought I'd dropped the f-bomb or slandered her family. I called myself every negative name in the book. I thought for sure she'd never want to talk to me again. I couldn't believe I'd made such an awful mistake. Ironically, in that very podcast, Sissy talked about how we can get fixated on something in our mind and remain on that one-loop roller coaster.

I began to realize that every time I made a mistake or didn't live up to my own standard of perfection, I believed I was the worst. I thought for sure Sissy wouldn't think I was a credible podcaster because of how I'd misspelled her name. I thought no one would listen to my podcast if I couldn't even spell correctly.

Around that time, I had a conversation on *Surviving Sarah* with my dear friend Rachel Macy Stafford. You may know her as the Hands Free Mama. Rachel shared a little phrase that had changed everything for her, and I knew it was what I needed to adopt for myself and for my girls:

Be kind to yourself. We all make mistakes.

That's where I started. Every time frustration or anger or shame or embarrassment rose up inside me because of something I had done, I stopped and said, "Be kind to yourself. We all make mistakes." But I didn't stop with myself. When my daughter would have an outburst and say she was the worst, I would immediately say, "Don't talk about yourself like that. That's not true. Be kind to yourself. We all make mistakes."

I had to start normalizing mistakes for my girls, and I had to start normalizing mistakes for myself. There was a season when that phrase "Be kind to yourself" was said on a daily basis. I felt like we were never going to get there—to that new way of thinking. But let me tell you about what happened one night while I was cooking dinner. You see, I've never claimed to be a great cook. In fact, for many years I shied away from trying because I was afraid of failing. I hated throwing away food I'd burned or meals that just didn't turn out. It made me feel like such a failure. I mean, who can't follow a recipe?

On this particular night, I had prepared something and burned it. Frustrated with myself, I exploded: "Ugh! Why do I always do this? I am the worst!" Then my younger daughter looked up at me and said, "It's okay, Mama. We all make mistakes. Be kind to yourself."

There it was. A new way of thinking. Failure didn't mean gold stars were taken away. Failure was simply a part of being human. And the best way to be human is to be kind. So I reframed things. *I failed at cooking dinner tonight, but I am not a failure.* There is a difference between something we did and something we are.

We have to train the voice in our head to speak with compassion, the way we would talk to a friend. And we have to help our children do this too. When they mess up or get frustrated with themselves, ask them what they would say to a friend. Then have them say it to themselves.

When you look in the mirror and don't like what you see, be kind to yourself.

When you are passed by for the promotion, be kind to yourself.

When you burn dinner again, be kind to yourself.

When you fail to close the deal, be kind to yourself.

When you miss the event, be kind to yourself.

Start with you. Let your kids watch you show yourself kindness. Let them see you talk to yourself the same way you would talk to a friend.

And when they mess up, fail the test, or spill the milk, say, "Be kind to yourself. We all make mistakes," or "We all have moments when we disappoint ourselves. It will be okay." Mistakes and unmet expectations don't define who we are. They're just a part of being human. Maybe we should start giving ourselves gold star stickers when we fail as a simple reminder that we all makes mistakes but it will be okay.

Henry James said, "Three things in human life are important: the first is to be kind; the second is to be kind; and the third is to be kind." Let's make kindness—including kindness to ourselves—a key building block of our kids' and our own identity. When we live out of a place of kindness toward ourselves, where we truly believe our identity is not based on our behavior, we can pass that kindness on to others.

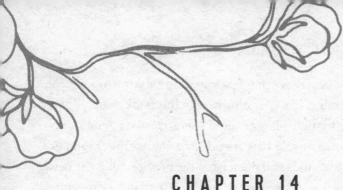

CHAPTER 14

YOU ARE VALUABLE BECAUSE YOU ARE YOU

It was a spring day in Georgia. The weather was finally warm again and summer was on the horizon. My girls were finishing up preschool and first grade. Since we were nearing the end of the school year and the weather was perfect, I thought it would be a great idea to take the girls to the town square for ice cream. (Go ahead and place that gold star on my chart.)

We enjoyed our ice cream, but then it was time to go. Completely reasonable for us to leave, to head home. But my older daughter, who was six at the time, took my suggestion to leave as a complete attack on her well-being. She flat-out refused to go, which meant it was time to battle. I started walking to the car (we weren't parked close) and she followed behind, screaming at the top of her lungs for the entire town to hear. Parenting is such a peach.

The following day at school pickup, I was talking to a couple of moms. And much like I'm doing here in this book, I shared this story from the battlefield. One mom was a trusted friend in my tribe, but the other was a new friend. As I shared the traumatic experience, my wounds still open from the previous day, the new friend said, "Well, my Grace would never do that. But we're pretty strict on her."

I think I just stared at her as if I were a deer caught in the headlights. All I heard in her response was that my daughter's behavior was a direct reflection on my inability to parent. If I were stricter, my daughter wouldn't have thrown a tantrum in public.

As moms, we hear this kind of message on a daily basis— the message that our kids' behavior is a direct reflection on our ability to parent. If our kids behave well, get good grades, and participate in all the activities, then we are good parents. If our kids throw tantrums, disrespect adults, or fail math, then something is wrong with us as parents.

But we all know that isn't how it actually works. No matter how many books I read, no matter how many tricks I tried, I had no control over my daughter's actions. At the end of the day, she was a human who made her own decisions.

As moms, we tend to attach our worth to a scale. When our kids misbehave, the scales tip out of our favor. But when they *do* behave, the scale tips back in our favor. We feel good about ourselves. We feel valuable. We feel like we're doing a good job.

But we don't just measure our value by our kids' behavior. Social media—I'm looking at you, Instagram—has the power to tip the scales, too. When you post the highlight reel of your life, including all the ways your kid cleaned up after herself, was kind to her siblings, and even led sixty-eight stuffed animals to Jesus, we feel good about our worth as a mother. We post these moments, hoping to see those hearts clicked. And with every heart clicked, we feel our value going up. But then we scroll through the beautifully curated feed of a friend and immediately find ourselves feeling less-than.

- Her kitchen is spotless and yours has spaghetti sauce splashed all over it.
- She looks put together and you're wearing sweatpants, your hair is unwashed, and your teeth are unbrushed. (And did you even remember to put on deodorant?)
- She somehow has time for a side hustle, even though she has three kids, and you can't even remember to take out the trash on the right day.
- Her daughter shows up to preschool with a smocked dress and a bow in her hair while your kid looks like you picked her up off the street just before school.
- Her husband praises her on social media, calling her a Proverbs 31 woman, and your husband forgot your birthday . . . again (true story).

But here's the deal about all these things—they are ever-changing. And they are external, based on the best or worst parts of someone else. Because of the number of likes on my Instagram post or whether or not my kids performed well, I could feel valued, loved, and accepted one moment and completely not the next.

Here's what raising my girls has taught me. When we allow our value to be based on anything external, we will always lose. Whether it's how our child behaves, what someone else is doing on social media, or what other people think of us, we lose when we base our value on it.

I came to see that what I believed to be true for my girls wasn't the same as what I believed to be true for me. I believed my girls have value because they exist. They live and breathe. No one can give them any more value than they already have. I still saw value in them even when they misbehaved, so why did I think the standard was different for me?

You and I are valuable no matter what. You and I are valuable even when we mess up or our kid messes up. Know this: you are still a good mom, a good wife, a good human worthy of love and acceptance even if those truths aren't confirmed by external measures. But knowing that and believing it to be true isn't easy. The battlefield of parenting is fierce, and it is the strongest external measure that I've experienced.

We have lived in a small downtown suburb of Atlanta for years. Our first neighborhood was right off the town square, within walking distance of stores and restaurants, and every person and every house on the street were eclectic in their own way. It was beautiful.

Our second rental house was in a gated community where every house was a cookie-cutter version of the others. It was very different from our first house. My girls have always been front-yard people. In our house on the eclectic street, my girls would hang out in the trees in the front yard so they could talk to every person and dog walking by. But our new house didn't really have a front yard. People pulled into their driveway, parked their car in the garage, and never set foot in the front yard unless they were getting the mail. This new setup was quite a shock to my girls. We had heard that the neighborhood was full of kids their ages, but we hadn't seen a single one. It had been five months, and my girls still didn't have any friends in the neighborhood.

That eventually changed when they saw a little girl outside riding her bike and pounced on her, ready to make a new friend. From that day on, they played with their new friend every single day. And in a snowball effect, playing with this one friend led to playing with more neighborhood kids. Finally, we felt a step closer to being connected in this neighborhood . . . until one December afternoon.

There was a knock at the door, and when I opened it, a woman I'd never seen before stood in front of me. She introduced herself as the mom of some of the boys in the neighborhood. In fact, her house was just behind ours.

She seemed stern and cold with her introduction, which threw me a little. Then she proceeded to show me a note she'd found in her mailbox. The note, scribbled in crayon, said, "Better watch out! A killer is on the loose!" She believed one of my girls had written the note, which, from the looks of it, appeared to be correct (we all know our kids' handwriting). Taking a cue from her demeanor, I apologized and validated her concern. "I am so sorry they did this. You are so right—this is unkind, and I will handle it with my kids." Keep in mind, my girls were elementary age with no prior criminal record (cue eye roll). I asked if I could keep the note so I could show it to my girls. She reluctantly handed it over and left.

I walked upstairs, showed Scott the note, then called the girls into the room. I asked why they'd done this. Their response was simple. All the kids, including this woman's boys, had been playing cops and robbers. The note was just a part of the game. I told them, "I totally understand, but it's not wise to talk about killers being on the loose. That could scare people if they didn't know you were playing a game. Their mother was very hurt and concerned by it. To make it right, you need to write an apology letter to their family."

I felt like I'd handled the situation well. But then there was another knock at the door, no less than ten minutes after the first one.

I opened the door to see the same neighbor. She firmly asked for the letter back because she needed to show it to her husband. When I questioned why, she answered that she wasn't sure whether she would need to take action against us. I said, "I thought we were good." She quickly replied, "I don't know you, so I don't know if we're good."

Well, that escalated quickly.

Basically, she needed to determine if my kids' action warranted calling the cops. Stop—hold the phone. I immediately started sweating and stumbling over my words. I had no clue how to respond. I'd never had such a confrontational conversation about my kids.

She met me with shame and judgment. Your kids aren't good. You aren't good.

I about died. I handed the note back, walked into the house, and completely lost it. Parenting is the most uncertain and vulnerable thing I've ever done in my life. I feel like I mess up more than I get it right. So when someone met my vulnerability with shame, it's no wonder I broke down.

This experience highlighted the false belief that my worth, my value, is tied to externals. I had believed that my worth was tied to my kids' behavior and my ability to parent. The fact that someone would question my parenting to the point of calling the police cut me deep.

News flash: parenting ain't easy. And, friends, we are all fighting a difficult battle. We show up every day trying to do our best. I expected that mother to meet me in a place of commonality. I expected her to know what it's like to raise kids who do dumb things. I expected her to understand that making mistakes is part of growing and learning. Instead, I was met with anger, suspicion, and shame. Those things don't build connection; they tear it down. That experience had the potential to devastate my belief in my value as a mother.

I tell you this story because it is so important to understand that no matter what, your value is not connected to your child's behavior or to any external person or circumstance. If that were true, if external measures were an indicator of my value, no doubt I'd be deemed the world's worst mom. Someone would have handed me that trophy on Mother's Day. I have kids who did something dumb enough to cause another family to want to call the cops on them. Surely I must be a bad mom.

But I've been on a journey to believe something different. I don't want to see my value as a scale that can tip one way or the other. We have to start believing that we are valuable because we exist in this life.

Can I tell you something? Changing a negative belief about ourselves doesn't happen overnight. We have days where we look to outside sources to determine our value. We look to friends, social media, business successes, and our kids' behavior to measure how we're doing. And we almost always come up short. But on those days when we remember that our value isn't based on anything we do or anything someone says about us, we discover an inner strength and peace.

The truth is, *you are valuable because you are you*. Nothing needs to be done to you, said about you, or validated on your behalf. We see how valuable our kids are—how nothing they could do, say, or think would ever change their value in our eyes. Yet somehow we hold ourselves to a different standard.

You have value even when your child throws an epic meltdown on the town square.

You have value even if your house never looks put-together.

You have value even though you can't drop a jeans size.

You have value even if your kid never makes the grades or the team.

You have value even when someone doesn't choose you.

You are valuable because you are you.

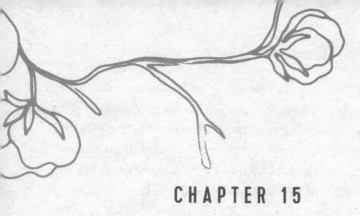

CHAPTER 15

YOU CAN TRUST
HER—YOUR BODY

When I was nine years old, a girl at a party called me fat. *Sarah's so fat!* I can still clearly remember the scene unfolding. At the time, it was as if I were watching my life from the outside looking in. Until then, I'd had no worries about my body. I truly didn't notice it. I was just a kid. I ate cereal for breakfast and loved ice cream, but in no way was I worried about how my body looked. But that day my body let me down and left me out, so I learned not to trust my body.

For nearly two decades after that, I hated my body because I felt like it had failed me, betrayed me. I had learned that my body was the measure by which I would be accepted, admired, or included. Whether that was actually true or not, it was *my* truth. I starved myself. I threw up. I exercised. I dieted. I did it all. And let me just tell you, living that way was exhausting.

Now that I have girls, I can't help but want something different for them. My girls are the ones who shook me out of the spiral of self-destruction that had been going on since before they even existed. When I was in my early twenties, I went to my mentor's house one night after work, and as we sat together on her sofa after her young children had gone to bed, she listened to me go on and on about how I felt about myself. I must have sounded like a broken record as I told her my struggles. Finally, she stopped me, looked me in the eyes, and said, "For the sake of your future children, you have to stop. They will treat food the way you do. They will treat themselves the way you do."

Cue mic drop.

Her words hit me powerfully. She was right. The idea of my future children jolted me out of my warped view of myself. I didn't have kids at the time and wasn't even dating anyone, but at that point, I realized I would be a mother someday, and my children would learn about their bodies by watching how I treated mine.

Even now, writing about body image is difficult for me because I don't have it all figured out. It's hard for me to admit that I still think about my body, my appearance, the food I eat, and my activity level far more than I wish. I must confess I still don't know what "normal" is supposed to be. I've spent thirty years of my life trying to learn, unlearn, and relearn things about my body.

I've tried to avoid the scale my entire life. The numbers that appear on it plague me. They define me in a way nothing else does. The other day, I stood on the scale, and the number I saw took my breath away a little. I weighed nearly fifteen pounds more than I'd weighed the previous year. But I'd been coaching myself about the scale. Before I stepped on it, I said out loud, "Don't be afraid of the number. Be brave. The number doesn't define your worth." No, that number wasn't what I wanted to see, but something dawned on me in that moment. Life felt the same that day as it did the year before. There was no real difference between me last year, fifteen pounds lighter, and me now. Friendships didn't change because of that number. My job didn't change because of that number. My children didn't stop loving me because of that number. My world didn't come crashing down because the number on the scale had changed. The essence of me was the same. What brought me joy was the same. What made me sad was the same. What excited me was the same. I was still me. The change in weight didn't change *me*.

I thought back and wished I'd appreciated how good I looked the year before. But I had also spent that year agonizing over the number on the scale and the size of my jeans. Just like little nine-year-old Sarah at the party, I couldn't see myself. I remembered the angst I felt. The sleep I lost over whether or not I should have eaten that dessert. The feeling that I still needed to strive for better self-control, for fewer pounds and inches. If only I had realized how good I looked. Maybe I would have relaxed and enjoyed where I was in life.

Now, at forty-two, I'm working on enjoying where I am in life. I'm working on being okay with the number on the scale and the size of the jeans I wear. Because maybe, ten years down the road, I'll be thinking, "Man, I would love to be back at the size I was when I was forty-two. I should have enjoyed it." Aging is hard. Seeing how quickly ten years go by and how quickly our appearance changes is not easy. We need to learn to love where we are. We need to learn to love the bodies we have.

That day on the scale, I realized I needed to start appreciating my body. But more than that, I needed to start *loving* and even *liking* my body. I didn't want my girls to struggle to appreciate and love their own bodies. Here is the truth we've talked about in every chapter: I discovered that when I want something for my girls, I want it for myself, too.

I want my girls *and myself* to love our bodies.

I want my girls *and myself* to learn to trust and appreciate our bodies.

I want my girls *and myself* to believe that our bodies are good and are *for* them.

I thought about what helped me love and appreciate others. It was empathy. But until then, I had only thought about empathy toward others. I hadn't thought about it in regard to myself. I knew I could hold a belief about someone, but meeting someone in person changed everything. For example, I could think that being a Yankees fan is abominable until I got to know a fan personally. Yes, that's a lighthearted example. But this idea applies to bigger things, too. I could think that being gay was wrong until I became friends with someone who was gay. Or I could think that holding a different political view or religious faith makes someone wrong until I get to know that person up close. Knowing someone makes everything personal. It reminds us that we're all human.

I decided to treat my body like a friend, like someone I knew—to make it personal. To help me do this, I adopted a new way of thinking about my body. I started referring to my body as *she*. She is me. I'm not sure why I never saw that. Maybe it goes back to learning to be kind to yourself, to speak to yourself like you would speak to a friend. Maybe it goes back to the idea that when you meet someone in person, you have a hard time hating them. I had to start seeing my body as she, as Sarah.

I spent so much time criticizing her, but she has served me extraordinarily well. She's had no broken bones. She's played sports and run races. She's carried two babies to full term and endured great measures to bring them into the world. She's recovered from two C-sections. She can jump on trampolines, do cartwheels, and ride scooters around the block with her kids. She walks the neighborhood every day. She uses her arms to hug and love those around her. Her smile has the ability to light up a room. She's lived and breathed and moved for over forty years. She is strong.

She is good.

As I began learning to love my body, I found that part of my problem was that deep down, I didn't believe she was good. Until this point, I believed I shouldn't trust my body. Somewhere along the way, I interpreted that my body was flawed—full of sin, even. I figured that anything of myself was wrong, shouldn't be trusted, and needed salvation. Because of my warped thinking, I spent years second-guessing her.

But now I see that our bodies are not flawed, full of sin, and in need of redemption. Our bodies are physical. Our bodies are beautifully complex and exist to protect us. I spent a good chunk of my life trying to drown out the voice screaming from within—my inner voice. That voice, my gut, really, was trying to help me. It wasn't trying to harm me but to protect me. Yet I thought I wasn't supposed to trust my gut.

When we feel something in our gut, it's trying to tell us something. It's asking us to pay attention. We can struggle with this no matter our age. My girls have thought something was wrong with their bodies because they had big, negative emotions. Any negative emotion caused them to question if something was wrong with them. But as I learned to trust my own body, I started telling them that their emotions are there good. Emotions are their bodies' way of trying to protect them from potential harm. Emotions are their bodies' way of helping them feel what other people feel. I told them that their emotions are their superpowers.

Rory has the ability to feel sad with people. She can sense when someone might need support. Or when Sinclair feels afraid or nervous or anxious, I remind her that her body is tuned in to her surroundings. All good things.

Almost every day of the first week of middle school, Sinclair said she felt sick to her stomach. She felt nervous. Instead of encouraging her to dismiss those feelings, I wanted her to realize how her body was trying to look out for her. So I said, "That's your body's way of telling you to pay attention. It's normal. That's your body taking care of you. It wants you to look around and see if you need to escape or if you have what you need to be okay. *You can trust her—your body.*"

One of the biggest areas in which we're conditioned not to trust our bodies is the area of sexuality. I want my girls to learn that they *can* trust their bodies with sexuality because I grew up thinking I couldn't trust mine in that area. I don't want my girls to fear their sexuality. I want them to be able to trust what is inside—to trust her. And listen, talking about my girls' sexuality is just as uncomfortable for me as it is for you. What helps is stepping back and imagining them at twenty, thirty, or forty. What do I want for them? How do I want them to view their bodies and their sexuality? Do I want them to be afraid? Do I want them to be polite and do what others want them to do? Or do I want them to figure out who they are and what they want and to learn to trust themselves? I want the latter, for sure.

Early on, Scott and I decided to start talking about sexuality with our girls. We wanted conversations about sex to be as normal as possible. I still remember the first conversation. Rory was four and Sinclair was six. We sat on the floor in front of their bunk beds with a book written by my friend Jim Burns titled *God Made Your Body*. Each page talked about our bodies. It called everything by name and even talked in the simplest of ways about sex. I remember telling myself to just keep my eyes on the pages and read. (I'll admit, I downed a margarita before having this conversation. Sometimes a little liquid courage is necessary.) We spoke about vaginas the same way we spoke about elbows. Part of their body. But at the same time, I wanted them to know that all of their body (elbows included) is theirs. Not someone else's. They are the boss of their body. They are to care for it and enjoy it. Their body doesn't exist for someone else, but for them. Private parts are private, not public. And if someone wants to see those private parts without their permission, it's not okay.

I wish I had known that. I found myself in situations as a child where people asked to see certain parts of my body. I was young and didn't know any better, and wanting to be polite, I complied. I wish I'd known I was the boss of my body and that my private parts were just for me.

When we shy away from having conversations about sex with our kids, we set them up for future shame, confusion, and mistrust. We didn't want to have a one-time conversation when they were thirteen. Instead, we started early and have conversations often. The door is always open for their questions, even if they sometimes arrive at inconvenient times. Once, when our neighbors were over for a barbecue, one of my girls asked exactly how sex happens. We've had conversations about oral sex when all of us, Scott included, were in the car driving to visit the girls' grandparents. Sometimes the questions come while washing the dishes or taking a walk around the block. Often, the girls will circle back around out of the blue and ask, "Do I really have to do that thing in order to have a baby?" For now, both girls are standing firm in the adoption camp. And it's normal and even good that they feel that way. They're young. But one day, I would be concerned if they weren't interested in and excited about sex. That would be a red flag. They don't need to be afraid of what they feel inside their bodies.

Raising my girls to have a healthy sexuality forced me to look at my own view of sexuality. Just as I didn't trust my body when it came to my appearance, I didn't trust her with sex. I was a teen-ager in the '90s when purity culture entered the scene. I believed that true love waited and that any sexual feelings I had needed to be squashed. I spent my adolescent years and my early twenties learning to suppress myself. Purity culture had created shame in me, and I carried that shame until I was forty years old—and I'd been married for nearly fifteen years by that point! The last thing I want my girls to feel when it comes to their bodies is shame about their sexuality.

I spent so many years not trusting myself that it took me equally as long to learn *to* trust myself with my sexuality. For many people, me included, it's hard to spend decades avoiding everything about sexuality and viewing it all as wrong unless you're married, then flip the switch just because you've said I do. I had a hard time unlearning that concept. Living our lives in fear is unhealthy, but that is exactly what purity culture teaches—fear.

Now hear me: I don't think my girls are old enough for sex. I want them to wait for as long as possible. I want to make sure that as I talk to them about the reasons not to have sex—the consequences it can bring—I also talk to them about responsibility. About wisdom. About viewing sexuality as a good thing. About listening to their bodies. About what integrity looks like in this department.

For us, much of this comes down to helping our kids by teaching to ask critical questions about it. Questions like "Why do I want to do this?" and "Is there mutual love, trust and respect?" and "Would it hurt to wait longer?" and "Is this the wise thing to do in light of my past decisions, present circumstances and future hopes and dreams?" (Thanks to Andy Stanley for asking that in a sermon many years ago—it stuck in my mind.) This is how our kids develop the ability to listen to themselves and to wisdom. They still may choose something that I wouldn't choose for them, but we have to remember that even if they choose something different than what we would want for them, it is *their* story. We can't prevent them from ever feeling and experiencing shame, but we can prevent unnecessary shame. We can help them remember that their behaviors don't define their identity. I don't want my kids to feel shame from me, Scott, or the church, because sexual shame can be some of the worst shame to carry. My hope is that my girls learn how to handle vulnerability with courage and that if they do experience shame, they will rise above it.

I want our kids to listen to themselves and to listen to wisdom. The whole conversation around sex is a complicated subject. What is wise for a fifteen-year-old may not be the same as what is wise for a forty-year-old. When it comes to my teenage girls, waiting for sex until marriage is a wise choice. It protects from many things that could cause pain, hurt, or shame. But I want to be mindful about the reality in which we live so that I don't create unnecessary shame.

Many years ago, when our girls were little, I was studying research about what life is like for teenagers specifically around sexuality. I didn't want us to be parents who wore rose-colored glasses about what life was really like or would be for our daughters. Statistics show that an estimated 55 percent of teens have had sex by age eighteen.[1] As parents, we wanted to face this topic with the reality of the world in which our girls live—there is a 55 percent chance they will have sex before they even graduate high school—let alone before getting married. I knew so many people growing up who got married young simply because they really wanted to have sex but knew they should wait until marriage for it. With all that in mind, I posed a question to Scott: "Would you rather them marry a jerk (I used a much harsher word) who isn't good for them just to have sex, or give them permission to have sex before marriage?" Both of us, without skipping a beat, chose sex before marriage. That's because we know that sex isn't the end-all. At the time, I had no idea this question would set us on a trajectory of taking note of how being raised in purity culture had affected our sexuality and figuring out how to raise sexually healthy humans. But when you're raised in purity culture instead of a culture of sexual integrity, sex *is* the end-all of relationships. Purity culture values it more than anything, using it to measure one's spiritual commitment, one's closeness to God. In essence, purity culture has put sex on a pedestal. But sex doesn't belong on a pedestal, nor should abstinence from sex be viewed as a badge of spiritual honor. Remaining sexually pure is not the highest way to honor God. Being a virgin at marriage doesn't make you more valuable. Virginity isn't the greatest gift you can give your future spouse. The greatest gift you can give your future spouse is your commitment, your trust, your truest self.

That's why it's so important to learn to trust yourself. When I believe that my body is good and is for me, I am able to show up in a more authentic way in my relationships. I spent too many years silencing my body and not trusting her. I pitted her against God. I thought that if I wanted it, maybe it wasn't right. If I wanted it, my gut wanted it, and my mind wanted it, then it probably wasn't what God wanted for me. And how could I figure out the difference between what he wanted and what I wanted?

Even the creation story points toward how we should view ourselves in this world. When God created mankind, it was good. If God created us and said we were good, maybe we could start there when it comes to trusting ourselves. We so quickly jump to Genesis 3, where the author describes the fall of man, that we forget that God saw us as good. I want my girls to be able to trust themselves—to see themselves as good. To stand in new and unfamiliar situations and listen to themselves. To pay attention to what their bodies are trying to tell them. To believe that their bodies are for them, not against them. To understand that the wants and desires inside them aren't inherently evil.

I wish I had learned earlier to trust my body. She's not bad. She's not evil. She's my biggest ally. She deserves some love.

Your body has done a great job on your behalf. So instead of complaining about her, examining her with a critical eye, wishing she looked different, mistrusting her every decision, maybe you could smile at her in the mirror. Maybe even say, "thank you." Maybe, just maybe, you could start enjoying her as you learn to trust her.

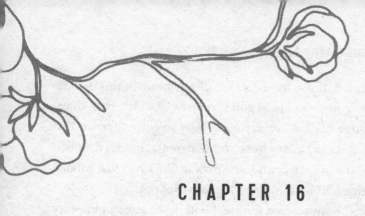

CHAPTER 16

DON'T *SHOULD* YOURSELF

I used to believe potty training was possible and achievable. Sinclair was not yet two-and-a-half years old, and Rory was just a squishy little newborn. Scott was in a season of work that was incredibly fun for him. His job took him all around the world capturing stories and video footage. As he prepared for an upcoming trip to Israel, I thought I could have some "fun" of my own. I decided this would be the perfect opportunity for potty-training boot camp. If you've never heard of this, let me explain. You basically lock yourself in your home for three days, and by the end of it, your kid uses the potty. Sounds easy, right? *Nope.*

My girl had given me zero indication that she was ready to— or even remotely eager to—use the potty, yet I was determined to make it happen because, after all, two-year-olds are *supposed to* be potty trained. If you have ever felt like a failure in this department, please know you are in good company. I didn't even make it the full three days. After day one, I was so entirely frustrated that I packed up my kids, drove to my parents' house, dropped them off on the doorstep, and drove away like I had just robbed a bank. I am a potty-training boot camp dropout.

And now? I am scarred for life. I will never attempt to potty train a child again. (Side note: I was so scarred that I didn't even attempt to potty train Rory. I dropped her off at preschool and lied that we were working on it. They had her trained by the end of the week.)

So why did I attempt potty training when my daughter showed no signs of readiness? Why did I believe my own personality would respond well to a boot camp–style effort? Because I believed I was *supposed to*. Isn't that like so much of life? We often find ourselves in the middle of something or contemplating something simply because we believe we are supposed to.

I've done a lot of things in life because I was *supposed to*:

Dating a certain guy
Getting married at a certain age
Having kids at a certain age
Buying a house
Going to a certain school
Being part of a certain group
Volunteering at certain events
Getting a dog
Walking said dog
Loving said dog (clearly I have some unresolved issues
    around our dog)

So many things happened in my life because I felt like I was *supposed to* do them. And many of them I didn't even think long about because of the sheer obligation I felt. I had lived so long in supposed-to land that I couldn't recognize what I wanted or needed. I only saw what I was supposed to do.

Why is that? For me, a voice in my head tells me that love and acceptance are tied to each other and serve as the end goal of each choice I make. I always saw each decision as a choose-your-own-adventure scenario, except with the end goal as love and acceptance. And I desperately wanted to be accepted—to the point where I was willing to do whatever I was *supposed to* do in order to gain that acceptance. I reached a point where I didn't even know up from down unless it involved the words *supposed to* or *should*. I had coasted in life, pleasing and performing for others. And honestly, I got far doing that, but at what cost?

I lost sight of who I am.

And I started to feel more and more resentment.

I found that when I did things because I was *supposed to*, I ended up feeling resentment toward others, toward myself, and even toward God. Always listening for *should* and *supposed to* kept me from hearing what I really wanted. I stopped doing what I wanted to do and did what I was supposed to do. Before long, I lost confidence in myself. By living in should-land, I lost the ability to do even the smallest thing based on what *I* wanted.

I questioned all my decisions and lived in fear of doing the wrong thing. I was afraid that certain decisions wouldn't be biblical enough, spiritual enough, right enough. I worried about disappointing others with my decisions. What if I made someone unhappy? What if I didn't do what someone else wanted? I was conditioned to please, but the more time I spent pleasing, perfecting, and keeping the peace, the more I doubted everything I wanted and everything I didn't want. And resentment built up like a wall around my heart.

Nothing highlighted my tendency to "should" myself more than motherhood. My child was the ultimate person to please, to perform for, to keep the peace with. If I performed right, maybe she wouldn't cry. If I did what everyone told me I should do with regard to sleep schedules, vaccinations, and discipline, then I would be a good mother. I struggled to do what I felt was right for me and often chose to listen to what others said I should do instead.

The more I mothered, the more I aged, the more I started to pay attention to the inner dialogue in my head. If I heard myself say, "I should do this," or "I'm supposed to do that," I would flag those moments in my mind. Then I asked myself questions and got curious about why I felt and thought that way.

Here's a silly example. I hinted earlier in the chapter as to how I feel about my dog, Murray. I love to take walks and, as you recall, I use walks as my smoke breaks to get out of the house, clear my head, and breathe. But when I walk Murray, I often return feeling more unsettled than when I left. My arms ache from controlling all ninety-five pounds of my dog, because he is terrible on a leash. (Please don't judge my value by my puppy parenting skills.) So I find myself cussing out and flipping off neighborhood dogs. Walking Murray is not life-giving. Walking him is the exact opposite of what I need.

But I *should* walk him.

He is *supposed to* have exercise.

I'm *supposed to* be the one who gives him that exercise.

A good dog owner *should* walk her dog.

I heard myself saying those things over and over to myself, so I checked it. And I realized I was only walking Murray because I felt like I was *supposed to*—like I *should*. Do you know what I did? I stopped. I decided to take Murray for a walk only when I wanted to. And you know how that felt? Freeing. Silly, right? But the lesson rings true. The more I practice paying attention to the *shoulds* in the small parts of my life, the more equipped I am to discern the *shoulds* in the big things.

It all comes down to giving ourselves permission to do what we want to do or not do what we don't want to do. Permission to trust the voice inside us. Permission to pay attention to ourselves.

This shows up in motherhood all the time. I felt like I should nurse my babies. I felt like the consensus around me affirmed that choice. But nursing babies, for me, was completely misery-inducing. Tiny baby Sinclair fought me every time I nursed. I could only hold her in one position, which wasn't a natural one. I felt like I experienced a sensory overload in response to nursing. But I kept on because I felt like I was supposed to. This isn't an argument about whether or not nursing your baby is right. It just wasn't right for me, and I wish I had paid attention to that sooner.

As my kids aged, this showed up in decisions about school. There was immense pressure surrounding where to send kids to school. Parents face pressure as early as preschool because "where you send your kids to preschool will determine where they go to college." Talk about pressure! When Sinclair entered elementary school, we lived in a quaint downtown community with walkable streets leading to the elementary school. However, many families didn't want to send their kids there because the academic ratings were low. I wrestled with what to do. I felt like I was supposed to send my kid to a highly ranked school, but deep down, I just wanted to send her to the neighborhood school. It was the most convenient. In the end, my choice isn't any more right than someone who chose to send their kid to the top ranked school. It was about thinking about what was best for us. The point is to pay attention to what *should*s we hear and then hold it up to what we really want to do. To be true to ourselves, we need to listen to ourselves. We have to put the *should*s aside.

It's one thing to decide not to walk the dog or go to a certain school, but what about bigger things?

I grew up going to church twice on Sundays and again on Wednesdays. If the doors were open, my family was there and loved it. A couple of years after college, I found myself working for a church. And then after about six years of working full-time for churches, I transitioned to helping those who lead churches. I created, wrote, and produced curriculum for a Christian nonprofit. Church had always been a major part of my life.

But over the last few years, things changed for me. I felt tired and noticed that our family had very little time together, especially time to rest. We would walk into the church building on Sunday morning and separate, all going in different directions for each of us to experience our own service. I started to dread going every week. I felt frustrated and critical. Resentment was starting to build up around my heart. In any other scenario in life, I wouldn't hesitate to stop participating in something that brought out such negative feelings, but this was different. This was church. I'm *supposed to* go to church. It's what Christians *should* do.

I found myself trying to figure out a way around going to church. My husband had been trying to convince me for years to live on a sailboat. Maybe that was the answer! Because if we lived on a boat, nobody would question why we didn't go to church. They would say, "Oh, of course you don't go to church. You live in the middle of the ocean. The ocean is your church."

That's when I started to pay attention to *why* I was feeling so unsettled. Deep down, my gut said that our family needed time away from church. We needed to rest. We needed the opportunity to spend more time together as a family. I took note of all the *shoulds* and *supposed tos* and then made a decision.

I gave myself permission to stop going to church for a season.

Instead of feeling resentment about going to church, I found peace in not going. Our family experienced more peace, more rest. On Sundays, we try to spend intentional time together. Some days we hike. Some days we drive somewhere to experience something different. And some days we simply rest. It's important to give yourself or your family permission to do what is best for them for any given season.

The decision to stop going to church for a season wasn't easy. Some decisions are easier than others. Some decisions carry less judgment from the world around you. But life is too short to live for the expectations of others.

Another way to avoid resentment is to draw boundaries. Clear boundaries help you know what you are and aren't okay with.

In 2018, I did a few interviews for the podcast that I just didn't enjoy. In fact, I didn't fully agree with what my guests were saying, but I found myself in *should* land. I knew deep down that these guests wouldn't be a great fit for my audience, but I thought I *should* have these people on my show. I thought I was *supposed to* agree with them. And because I said yes when, deep down, I knew I should have said no, I felt resentment and anger. So the next year, I created some boundaries. I decided what kinds of guests and topics would be allowed and what wouldn't be allowed. And instead of resentment, I felt freedom. I was able to be true to myself.

Drawing boundaries allowed me to give myself permission to do what I knew was good for me to do. Think about what you love and enjoy and what you don't. Think about the expectations you're placing on yourself and determine whether they are causing you to feel resentment. Then give yourself permission to follow what you want to do. I don't think there is one right way to do things. We each have our own personality, temperament, and desires. What is true for me may not be true for you. What I want or need may not be the same for you.

Obviously, there are some things in life you *have* to do, like paying your rent (unless you don't mind being evicted). But there are plenty of other choices and opportunities in our lives that aren't designated right or wrong, black or white, up or down. That's where we need to lean in, pay attention, and listen to ourselves.

The same goes for our kids, too. I want my girls to become young women who listen to themselves, who pay attention to what they feel, who know who they are. I don't want them to do something simply because they *should*. I don't want them to do something simply because they are *supposed to*.

We can show our kids how to figure out what they really want and why they want to do something. We can teach them to ask questions of themselves. When it comes to their activities, we can ask them if this is something they really want to do, rather than just something all their friends are doing.

Do you want to join that small group?

Do you participate in that event?

Do you want to play basketball?

Do you want to be in the drama club?

What do *you* really want to do?

Ask these questions, and then give them permission to do what they want to do.

If I want anything for my girls, it's for them to be women who refuse to live in should land. Women who question what they are *supposed to* do. Women who stop and ask themselves what they really want and don't want. Women who are bold enough to be true to themselves, even if it means disrupting the peace or disappointing someone.

I hope to be that woman, too.

This is your one precious life. It is meant to be lived. It is meant to be experienced. Grief will follow if we get to the end of the line and realize that we never allowed the world to see the real us and never allowed ourselves to experience the world the way we wanted to.

As a woman, you face a never-ending list of *shoulds* and *supposed tos* as women. Don't forget about you. Don't forget about the girl in you. Listen to her—she's trying to tell you who she really is and what she really wants. Don't should yourself. Instead, lay down the *shoulds* and *supposed tos* and pick up freedom.

CHAPTER 17

YOU'RE NOT TOO PRECIOUS

Let me go on record to say that I am *not* a Pinterest mom. I'm not a crafty mom. And I'm not a room mom. I'm more of a let-me-pay-money-for-that-instead-of-paying-in-time kind of mom.

Experiencing elementary school in an affluent area, I realized quickly that there was practically a waiting list for people who wanted to be room mom, which allowed me to keep living my best non-Pinterest life.

And while elementary school is an opportunity for us to rise to the challenge of Pinterest, it is also a place where we feel a great need to protect our precious children. Many of us seem to bubble-wrap our kids to send them to school. We're present for every event, every sneeze. We make sure they have the "right" teacher and peers in their class. And while our overprotective tendencies can show caring, they also add a layer of unhealthy insulation. For us, that meant a lot of fear accompanied the transition from that insulated place when it came time for middle school. Middle school already gets a bad rap—and rightfully so. Many of us can trace our most difficult moments back to middle school.

At the middle school open house, word on the street was that the lockers were pretty intense. Meaning some foul language was likely to be scribbled inside them. There were even rumors that the PE teachers cussed (shocker). Now, my girls have heard me cuss. Not only have they heard me cuss—and not apologize about it—but we also had a crash course in all the swear words when they were around eight or nine years old. I remember sitting in the car at a traffic light, saying all the words. It was quite funny.

So when my girl heard about the bad words written in the lockers and the teachers who might swear, I looked at her and said, "You are not so precious that you can't handle a few cuss words." We have got to learn to take the bubble-wrap off our kids. They live in a real world with real people. And they can handle more than you think.

Parents experience a lot of angst about where to send their kids to school. It seems like everyone has an opinion about what is best. And at root of most of these opinions is fear. Will they make friends? Will this school set them up for success? Will they suffer harm?

I didn't want fear driving my decision, but after receiving feedback from others, I thought, *Maybe they're right.* Maybe I was supposed to worry about those things. Maybe Sinclair was too precious to handle it. But my gut told me something different. My gut told me that's where we needed to be. My gut said we didn't need to make a decision out of fear that something bad might happen. And can I tell you something? Sinclair absolutely thrived at that school. When we take the bubble-wrap off our kids, we allow room for something magical to happen.

Really, at the root of overprotection—that tendency to swathe our kids in bubble-wrap—is fear. So much of parenting is wrapped up in being afraid of making the right choices for our kids. We carry so much pressure to do the best for them. Hence the bubble-wrap. We think if we just wrap them up carefully enough, they will be fine. But think about the ways in which you were bubble-wrapped as a kid. Did it help you? Did it shield you? Or did you ultimately rebel against it?

I think back to growing up in the Bible Belt in the '80s and remember that the message I heard over and over was that culture was bad. If you gave your eyes and ears to anything in culture, you were toast. I distinctly remember the day my mother threw out all our Smurfs and Care Bears. Gone. (We still laugh with her about that to this day.) At some point, she had heard someone talk about how dangerous those little blue creatures and fluffy bears were. But it didn't stop at Papa Smurf. My brother and I also couldn't listen to secular music. Growing up, I only ever heard Psalty the Singing Songbook, Carman, and the Gaither Vocal Band. We spent hours in the car driving to and from the beach, listening to Moody Bible Institute on the radio the whole time. A real fear was being broadcast to my parents that culture was bad—it was too worldly.

And do you know what eventually happened? You guessed it—I secretly listened to secular music. *Gasp.*

And look, I theoretically turned out okay. The C+C Music Factory didn't completely derail my teenage years. I make light about my upbringing (no offense, Mom and Dad), but I want you to see that you aren't the only one to worry about the future of your kid. You aren't the only one to wonder how the things you allow them to read, watch, listen to, or do today will ultimately affect their future.

We have to let our kids test out their wobbly legs before they leave our house in pursuit of college or a career. Now is the time to undo the bubble-wrap so they can bump into things while they can still come home and talk about it and attempt to figure it out.

I can't tell you how many conversations I've had with my girls that have made me squirm. Uncomfortable conversations. Awkward conversations. They have brought up questions about sex that I don't think I asked until I was practically graduating high school. They've heard things at school, from friends, in books, in music, and on TV that might prompt us to rush to the store and buy toilet paper in preparation for quarantining ourselves from the outside world for the rest of their childhood. But these kids aren't so precious. They can handle more than we think.

What are you afraid of having your children hear or experience? What makes you want to bust out the bubble-wrap? Think about what those things might be, then write them down. Sometimes just getting the words out of our heads and onto paper helps diminish our fears.

Think about the kind of people you want your kids to be when they go to college or start their first jobs. That's one of the best pieces of advice I heard from a local elementary school principal. When I went to visit that school, she told me my family's race would be the minority. She also said her daughter, who was away at state school, had told her she was so glad she'd been educated in this public school system because it had showed her what the real world would look like. She'd been able to see how diverse the world actually is. She wasn't shocked when she went off to college and met all the other kids who hadn't been bubble-wrapped.

That's what I want for my girls. I want them to experience real life under my roof so that when they go away to live on their own, they aren't surprised at the lack of bubble-wrap in the world.

When I was twenty-one years old, I packed up my Honda Accord and moved to California to work for a church. I know my mom was probably dying inside. Afraid for me to live so far away from home. Afraid of what I might bump into out there. But she took off the bubble-wrap and let me go. However hard that was for my parents, the day came when I drove away from them. I didn't question whether I could handle it. I believed I could. That's empowerment.

Imagine the kind of empowerment our kids' generation would have if we collectively said, "You're not so precious. You can handle it."

The other day, I found myself complaining about something. From behind me, I heard Rory's little ten-year-old voice say, "Mama, you're not so precious." I giggled and said, "You're right." I asked her what she meant by that, and she said, "You can do it. You are strong enough to handle it." Friends, that's it. Our kids need to know that they are strong enough and capable enough to handle whatever life brings. And I need someone to come behind me and remind me that I am, too.

When we bubble-wrap our kids, we communicate to them that they aren't strong enough. That they can't do it. That they can't handle it. That their minds are too frail to hear something different than what we have taught them. But we empower them when we let them, within reason, experience the world. I don't know about you, but I want to raise kids who are strong and confident. Who are the essence of resilient and resourceful. Who, when they face obstacles, don't automatically give up or look to me for help. I want them to be adults who are not offended by the things that others say or do.

And isn't this the hope for ourselves, too? That we would walk confidently through life knowing that we are strong and capable? You are not as frail as you think. Think about all that you have overcome or walked through. You are stronger than you realize. You are not so precious. Believing this to be true is taking the first step to becoming a more resilient woman.

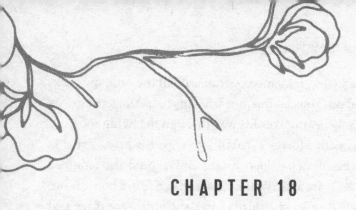

CHAPTER 18

THIS IS WHY WE CAN'T HAVE NICE THINGS

We have been renting houses for the last seven years. A certain pressure always seems to come with renting. Maybe you've never felt it, but for someone like me, who harbors perpetual anxiety about not messing anything up, renting with kids can be incredibly stressful. With each new rental house (at this writing, I'm sitting in our fifth one with kids), we've also had to pay a hefty pet deposit in case our dog destroys anything.

As I write, it is January, and it has rained no fewer than 871 days in the new year. Nothing but gray skies. Nothing but rain puddles. Nothing but mud in my backyard. Now, for many of you, mud in your backyard doesn't matter, but for us it does because of our dog.

Our dog, Murray, was the biggest regret of 2017. He has baseball bats for legs, weighs ninety-five pounds, and resembles a grizzly bear. Now, remember, because of all the rain, my back-yard is a mud pit. You can imagine what my house looks like once said ~~dog~~ grizzly bear makes his way through the living room.

But even with Murray's inability to wipe his paws, I've discovered that besides a pet deposit, landlords should also require a kid deposit. Kids are actually the ones who can ruin a house faster than a muddy dog. In our third rental, the girls were three and five. They destroyed that home in every way you can imagine: nail polish permanently painted on the hardwood floor, poop smeared on the walls (which I finally had to paint over), doors broken, curtain rods accidentally pulled down, leaving holes in the drywall. When we moved out, the house looked more like it had been occupied by frat boys than a family with two little girls.

This is where the great theologian Taylor Swift met me in my darkest moment and spoke a truth that forever changed my heart: "This is why we can't have nice things." Thank you, Taylor. You make me feel seen, heard, and understood.

But Taylor hasn't been the only pop culture influence in my life and motherhood. Pop culture has actually played a major role in my growing-up process. Let's go back in time to young Sarah.

As a kid, I was completely enthralled by pop culture. Maybe it was spending every Friday with one or the other of my grand-mothers. The two women rotated each week who kept me. When I was with my mom's mom, we always ate lunch at McDonald's. When I was with my dad's mom, it was Wendy's. Now, if you are a product of the '80s, you understand that the battle between McDonald's and Wendy's was quite intense. (I always wondered if the fast food battle between my grandmothers was about more than just hamburgers.)

Another battle was going on with what we watched. My mom's

mom always watched the ABC soap operas *Days of Our Lives* and *As the World Turns*. With my dad's mom, it was CBS's show *The Young and the Restless*. Why anyone thought it was age-appropriate for a child to watch these daytime dramas is beyond me, but I absolutely loved it. I created worlds for my Barbies based on the soaps. And then Friday nights always revolved around watching *The Dukes of Hazzard* and *Moonlighting*. It's no wonder I developed a love for pop culture.

I mentioned earlier that my parents tried hard to control my music. We were only allowed to listen to Christian music. Now, keep in mind, this was before the age of "worship" music. I'm talking Steve Green, Sandi Patty, Larnelle Harris, the Gaithers, Psalty the Singing Songbook, and of course Carman. Oh, Carman. He was my first culture crush. I genuinely thought I was going to marry him, and honestly, I'd say I had a chance since he remained single until he was practically a dinosaur. But I find it interesting how I was allowed to watch daytime dramas yet was forbidden to listen to Madonna, Michael Jackson, and Whitney Houston. Something didn't quite measure up.

Which led me to rebel and secretly listen to pop music. I remember turning on VH1, hoping to catch a glimpse of Amy Grant's music video for "Baby, Baby." I felt so rebellious. (Bless my heart.) I'd listened to the radio in my bedroom, recording on my boombox current hits like "Baby Got Back." Putting on my headphones in the car, I'd inject a cassette tape into my Walkman with contraband like C+C Music Factory, Technotronic, or the *Top Gun* soundtrack.

Pop culture was so much of who I was and who I wanted to be. It's not surprising that it's still an influence in my life today.

Just this week alone, I have felt so understood by pop culture.

It's a well-known fact in my family that I love Bill Murray. He's one of my top three people I'd love to meet, along with George W. Bush and Snoop Dogg. (Snoop Dogg is a story for another day, but trust me, it's a good one.) To me, parenting often feels like the plot from the Bill Murray movie *Groundhog Day*. You wake up to the same annoying soundtrack, experience the same things over and over, go to bed, and do it all over again the next day. This is especially true in the middle of a global pandemic. Every day you seem to do the very same thing, and nothing you do seems to matter.

There's also the movie *What about Bob?* Now, people either love this movie or hate it. If you hate it, I want to challenge you to watch it again with fresh eyes—eyes that see how this movie relates to being a parent. If you don't know the storyline, Bill Murray plays a man named Bob who is afraid of everything. His psychiatrist prescribes to him advice based on his book *Baby Steps*. He tells Bob that he needs to take a vacation from his problems so he can baby-step his way to overcoming his fears. I can't tell you how many times I've wanted to take a vacation from my problems. (If you didn't catch that, the kids are often my problem.)

But I usually don't get a vacation from my problems, and it's truly remarkable how many things I do wrong in this phase of parenting tweens. Now, let me clarify. I get that I'm not perfect— far from it. But I'm not talking about that. I'm talking about the things I get blamed for doing wrong that are actually things one of my daughters did. Forgot her homework? My fault. Lost her sweatshirt? Totally my fault. Failed a test? Again, somehow my fault.

I don't know what happens at your house, but these accusations fly out of my girls' mouths as if we're being filmed for a reality show. And while this is happening, a soundtrack plays in my head, telling me I need to calm down. I'm being too loud.

Again, thank you, Taylor.

Taylor isn't the only theologian who makes me feel understood. Bruno Mars is another favorite. On his album *24K Magic*, there's a song called "Perm" that my girls and I play on repeat. Judge me if you'd like, but there are some good parenting scripts tucked into those lyrics. The song is all about drama, and with girls, we have a lot of drama—a lot of emotions flying around at any given moment. Sometimes when we're in the heat of an emotional windstorm, I simply paraphrase Bruno: "Throw some perm on that attitude, girl! You need to relax."

Most of the time, my girls laugh when I say this, which actually breaks the storm.

There's one pop culture icon who I believe captures the essence of motherhood: Betty Draper from the show *Mad Men*. Here's what I love about Betty Draper. She represents a certain era of mothers. There once was a time when mothers just didn't care; they took things in stride. Most of the time, they didn't even know where their kids were! There was no app that enabled them to see where their kids were at any given moment. They simply seemed to have fewer cares in their world.

I remember having a conversation with my mom when I was feeling overwhelmed and flustered with a new baby. Drained by expectations, I was mentally, physically, and emotionally exhausted. How could a tiny human cause such angst? My mom said to me, "You just need to be like one of those smoking moms from the '60s. They just sat around with a cigarette in hand and didn't seem to have a care in the world." She was actually right. When I feel the pressure, it's helpful to remove myself from the situation, step outside into the fresh air, and breathe in and out. Smoking mom.

You see, pop culture—movies, television, books, music—has a way of helping us feel understood.

What would it be like to respond in the heat of parenting drama like Betty Draper? What if we pulled out our imaginary cigarettes and breathed in and out while removing ourselves from the pressure cooker moments?

What would it be like to take a vacation from our problems like Bill Murray's Bob? What if we started with something small, like enjoying a cup of coffee (or five cups like Lorelai Gilmore) or taking a walk with a friend or soaking in a bubble bath with your favorite book?

What if we allowed music to help us figure out how to parent our crazy tweens? (Thank you, Bruno and Taylor.)

Pop culture helped raise me in the formative years of my life, and it continues to raise me today. Through it, I've found voices that help me feel seen, heard, and understood. So look around. Look at movies, music, and books. Let them be an escape and a guide. We can lean in and take the advice. Taylor may be right about kids—this is why we can't have nice things—but I wouldn't trade the stories I've experienced from raising my girls.

CHAPTER 19

ME TOO

It feels like so many of us mothers are positioned against each other these days. Nothing can get a mother's blood boiling more than the topic of childbirth or nursing or vaccination or schooling. We tend to believe that our way is the right way. (News flash: Mothers aren't the only ones. Just look at the current state of America.) And we judge each other.

We look at the mother who chose to medicate during childbirth and we judge.

We look at the mother who chose not to vaccinate her child and we judge.

We look at the woman who chose to go back to work and we judge.

We look at the mother who chose to homeschool and we judge.

We look at the mother who lets her kids eat processed sugar and we judge.

Judgment is often our reaction when something bumps up

against what we feel is "right." The reality is, many aspects of motherhood feel weighty and scary. And anything we do as moms that feels uncertain carries the potential for judgment. The uncertainty of it drives us to create a story in our head that provides a solid rationale and a sense of rightness about what we've chosen to do. That's because we think certainty will make us feel better—it will make the shame, fear, and anxiety we feel dissipate.

Raising my girls has highlighted the part of myself that wants to judge, but it has also highlighted the tool I can use to move away from judgment—*empathy*. Empathy helps me see things from someone else's perspective. Empathy helps me see how other mothers are doing the best they can with the knowledge they have. Empathy helps me understand what it's like to feel disappointed, hurt, lonely, afraid, embarrassed. And because I can recognize those feelings in myself, I can better relate to others who feel the same way.

Empathy is like a tonic or a salve. It's a balm for our relationships with others. It gives us the ability to see life from a new perspective. Studies show that the more empathy we have, the more success in work and relationships we'll find. Empathy is exactly what we need to relate not only to our kids but also to the world around us.

But here's what's difficult: we are raising humans in a world where empathy is greatly lacking. Our world is a place dominated by "right" perspectives, where we tend to punish people for seeing the perspective of the other side. We are taught to live in a binary way—to see things as either black or white, right or wrong. But here's the interesting thing about the children in our homes: they are very receptive to learning how to see other perspectives. In fact, we're all born this way. We are wired to be curious. We are wired to feel what others feel. Brené Brown says, "Children are very receptive to learning perspective taking skills. They are naturally curious about the world and how others operate in it. They are also far less invested in their perspective being the 'right one.'"[1] (Except when it comes to siblings. My girls want to be right no matter what with each other.)

I spent a brief year working as a preschool director for a local church, and it never failed—if one baby started crying, they all started crying. We used to call that sympathy crying, but truly, it was empathy. We are born with the capability to feel what others feel.

Maybe that's why raising kids has provided the most teachable moments for my own growth in regard to empathy. Whenever I found myself in a vulnerable parenting moment, I hoped to God that someone would just understand how I was feeling. I hoped that instead of responding with judgment, they would respond with empathy. I hoped that they knew what it was like to feel lonely or disconnected or hurting or sad. I wanted to know I wasn't alone.

I wasn't the only one who struggled to know how to discipline.

I wasn't the only one who felt like an awkward middle schooler at curriculum night.

I wasn't the only one who was embarrassed by my child's behavior.

I wanted someone to reach out and say, "Me too."

I believe those are some of the most powerful words in our language. Those two words immediately allow us to drop the armor we wear. They enable us to be truly seen. They are like a thread that connects us together.

Here's why that little phrase is so important: Empathy paves the way for connection. Connection brings meaning in life. And where there is connection, judgment is almost impossible to feel. The greatest hope I have in parenting is that one day, when my girls are adults, we will have a strong connection, a real connection. A connection that allows them to show up as they are and know that their mother understands. That their mother knows what it feels like to feel pain, sorrow, fear, or disappointment. This kind of connection creates a safe place for them to land.

How do we develop this kind of connection?

Feel. Speak. Hear.

Empathy. Courage. Compassion.

First, we need to practice empathy—we need to learn to feel. The goal for ourselves and our children is to be people who can feel what others feel. Our children learn this ability when we flex the empathy muscle in front of them. I have a tendency to breeze through my emotions to get to the action. Action usually involves checking off a box, which is easier for me than dealing with feelings.

I remember a season in life when I was walking through great heartache and struggle. It felt like all the important relationships in my life were squeezing me. I decided to go see a counselor, something I had never done before. Her very first question was, "What are you feeling?" I was dumbstruck. I had no clue how to answer that question. I had never spent any time identifying what I felt below the surface.

As moms, we see our kids come home with all sorts of feelings to work out. When one of my girls comes home with big feelings, I tend to cut her off midway through her story with an action step that she should take. Usually my suggestion falls flat on the floor and the conversation becomes disconnected. My daughter usually leaves feeling unheard. But when I choose to respond intentionally, with empathy before action, the conversation is different. Eventually I may get to the action step, but the difference is that my daughter is ready to hear it after I've helped her identify what she feels and shared times when I've felt the same way. Our connection deepens because empathy leads to connection.

Some of the sweetest moments in parenting have been when my girls used empathy as a tonic for me. At the beginning of the pandemic of 2020, our friends' son died by suicide. These are friends whom we love and respect and look up to. Since we were under a shelter-in-place order at the time, the family had an online funeral. During the funeral, I just sobbed. I was heartbroken for my friends. And as I cried, my girls put their arms around me. They sat with me in the sadness. They didn't try to make light of what I was feeling. They didn't try to force me to take action. They just felt sad with me.

Sometimes we don't want our kids to see our pain, our hurt, or our sadness. We feel like we need to be the strong ones. But when we hide the hard parts of being human, we remove their opportunities to practice empathy.

One of the greatest gifts we can give to our kids—and ourselves—is the feeling of normalcy—the feeling of being connected, like they aren't the only one. You may not be able to fix what is going on, but you can always show up with empathy.

Here is what practicing empathy looks like for me. I tell my girls:

I understand.
That's hard.

That hurts.
Me too.
That's normal. It happens to me, too.
I know how you feel.
Tell me more.

The other day, Rory brought up how sometimes the drama among her friends is too much. It makes her feel sad. It makes her feel disconnected from her friends because she has to choose sides. My natural response would be to give a three-step action plan, but instead I chose to respond with empathy first. "That's hard. Tell me more about what happens." Sometimes we just need someone to continue the conversation so we can process out loud what's going on inside.

One of the benefits of leading a conversation with empathy is that it helps the other person to become a better problem solver. If I always swoop in with my three-step plan to overcome a situation, my girls will never realize that they have what it takes to solve the problem for themselves or to come up with their own conclusions about a situation. Asking questions allows them the space to process. Most of us as women naturally understand this. How many times have you poured out your feelings to someone of the male gender, only to be met with an action plan? Your response probably was, "I don't need you to fix this. I just need to vent and talk about it out loud." More times than not, as we talk and someone asks us questions and listens, we come to a conclusion on our own. We were looking for connection—empathy—not someone else's solution.

After we've learned to build connection by responding to others with empathy, we need to practice courage. This is when we speak. It takes courage to speak our story. We often think of courage as some grandiose act, but this kind of courage is ordinary.

One December night when Sinclair was in fifth grade, she seemed sad, quiet, and reserved when I picked her up from a Christmas party. As I inquired about what she was feeling and why, she told me how one of the girls at the party had said some hurtful things to her. I said, "That is hurtful. I can see why you feel sad. I had the same kind of thing happen when I was your age." Then I briefly told her about the friend who had called me fat at a party. She immediately felt connected when I said that. When we respond with empathy first, we validate what someone else is feeling. Then, when we have the courage to speak, we create a safe place for them to land.

Lastly, we can choose to practice compassion. This means hearing what others are really saying. Laying aside judgment and really listening. As I write this chapter, our country is experiencing a movement of compassion. The Black community has experienced wrongful deaths for far too long, and the time has come to say no more. What they have asked of the White community is for it to listen and to speak up—to practice compassion. Compassion recognizes that we have a shared humanity. When one hurts, we all hurt.

What would it look like if we worked to see life from another person's perspective? It would look like getting curious about their life. It would look like asking questions instead of making assumptions.

Empathy creates a softer response to the other person. Empathy weaves a common thread between the two of you, even though you may make different choices and live very different lives.

What would happen if we approached others with empathy instead of judgment?

What would happen if we listened to our kids with empathy first, before taking any other action?

What would happen if we approached those who are different from us with compassion?

We are works in progress. Empathy is a muscle we flex. The more we flex it, the more we practice it, the more we develop it. Being in relationship with people is one of the most vulnerable things we can do. But if we choose to show up for each other in those vulnerable places with empathy, then our lives, relationships, homes, work, and even country will be a better place. And it can all start by simply saying, "Me too."

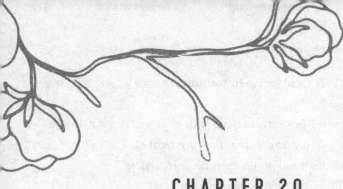

CHAPTER 20

BE A GOOD CITIZEN

Even if you aren't an anxious person, I'm willing to bet that you worry about some things. We have an amazing ability to create some wild stories in our minds based on our worries. And some of those wild stories begin not with the phrase, "Once upon a time," but rather, "What if . . . ?"

What if my newborn is spoiled from my holding her all the time?

What if my child doesn't go to this certain preschool?

What if she can't pass the seventh grade?

What if she dates a total lame butt? (You know I really wanted to say another word.)

What if she never grows up and leaves the house?

What if is often the soundtrack to a parent's mind, like a song on repeat except with every repetition our blood pressure rises and our fear increases. All of those what-ifs listed above are actual what-ifs from my own soundtrack, but let me tell you about one in particular.

What if I'm raising lazy, entitled kids who will one day move out and continue living as the slobs they are right now as tweens?

Will they be featured on an episode of *Hoarders*?

Will they be evicted from their apartments?

Will they ever learn how dishes actually get clean?

Will they figure out how to do their laundry?

Will they ever understand how the trash somehow disappeared from their home all those years?

Will they expect everyone around them to do everything for them?

Will they expect to be given every new updated technology device simply because they breathe?

What this record on repeat underscores is the need for our kids to learn how to care for the world around them. Part of my goal in raising kids is to raise good citizens. A citizen is simply someone who inhabits a place. I ultimately want my kids to grow up to be responsible, respectful, and caring citizens of their home, their belongings, their relationships, their community, their world, and even themselves.

To reach that goal, we have to start with the first place our kids inhabit—home. I started reframing how I talked with my girls about chores. We started talking about being good citizens of our home. When you are a good citizen of your home, you take care of it. You keep it clean. You pick up your space. You don't leave trash on the floor. You pick up after the dog. You don't write on the walls. You do all these things because you're a good citizen—because you care for what you have. Changing the language really helped us.

Caring for our space began to feel more like a team effort rather than one person's role.

Coming up with a system to prevent mayhem from happening in our home was no small feat. I looked at what I did to be a good citizen of our home and found that most of my efforts toward that end involve chores. I admit, I've struggled to figure out how to get my kids to take responsibility. I've spent countless hours on Pinterest, pinning all sorts of articles about teaching kids how to do chores and helping them learn to clean up after themselves.

And let me tell you, I've tried it all. We've done the allowance thing. We've done the work-for-hire thing. We've done the positive rewards thing. We've done the chore chart app thing. We've done the I'm-gonna-ground-you-until-eternity-if-you-don't-do-this thing. Nothing has really stuck. Yes, things get picked up, but sometimes the motivation is still lacking.

Can I be honest? I still don't have it fully figured out. Even as I type this, my daughter's room looks like a bomb went off. She puts clean clothes in the dirty clothes hamper to avoid putting them away. And towels still don't find their way to the hooks on the wall. We are clearly not mastering this area. Scott and I just keep hoping if we beat the drum long enough, good chore habits will stick one day. (Just for the record, our older daughter is twelve, if that gives you some relief in your own life.)

As I talked with my kids about being good citizens of our home, I looked around at the world—our earthly home. I took note of how I cared for it. And in small ways, I started to change. I started using fewer paper towels, swapped plastic containers for glass, and began recycling. I know it's not a lot, but it's something. And it models effort to our kids—effort to care for where we live.

One day your kids will grow up and live on their own. We don't want to raise kids who think they need to be paid to clean the house or mow the lawn or pick up after themselves. We want to raise kids who are motivated to be good citizens of what they have. And we do this by modeling for them how to care for the spaces we inhabit.

Being a good citizen goes beyond our home and the world around us, though. Good citizenship also applies to how we treat others and how we treat ourselves. If being a good citizen of our home is about caring for it and treating it with respect, what does that look like when it comes to the way we treat others and ourselves?

I thought about what kind of human I want to be and what kind of humans I want my girls to be.

Honest.

Kind.

Loving.

Brave.

Mindful.

Trustworthy.

Telling the truth in little things and in big things.

Being kind to others when they make mistakes—and being kind to themselves.

Loving others, even when it's hard.

Being brave when they feel big fears welling up inside.

Paying attention to the feelings and needs of others.

Being dependable and responsible members of their families and communities.

Rory came home one day and told me how her friend had sat all alone in the lunch room because her friend's best friend was absent from school that day. As Rory walked by, she decided to sit with the friend who was sitting alone instead of with her typical lunch friends. My heart soared because she chose to be a good citizen in that moment. She considered how she could care for someone who was lonely—even if it meant not sitting with her other friends. That is good citizenship.

I know it sounds sort of crazy to be a good citizen of yourself, but that's also important. In chapter 15 about our bodies, I mentioned that I tell my girls, "You are the boss of your body." This phrase applies to citizenship, too. I want my girls to grow up and not have to be reminded how to care for themselves. I put a Post-it note in their bathroom reminding them to brush their teeth, wash their hands, care for their contacts, wash their body, and wash their face. As my girls aged into tweens, they became overwhelmed with all they had to do to take care of themselves. (By the way, they loved the books from American Girl about taking care of their bodies.) But I wanted them to feel *empowered*. And I took advantage of the fact that many girls this age like to be bossy and in control. I leaned into it. "You get to boss yourself around. You are in charge. You are in control," I told them.

The same is true for me. Seeing myself as the boss of my body was helpful in learning to love my body. I am in control of caring for it. What does it need to be healthy? How can I care best for it? It's simple citizenship.

Being a good citizen isn't about being right or wrong. It's about caring for things—for the place you live and for the people you love. The goal in parenting is not to raise perfect humans. The goal is to raise humans who will love themselves, love others, and love the world in which they live.

CHAPTER 21

BE CURIOUS

Raising kids definitely makes a person well versed in kids' programming. Think about how much kid-oriented media you have consumed over the course of your parenting career. Enough to be considered an expert at this point? Quite possibly. Sinclair went through a phase when she was obsessed with *Yo Gabba Gabba!* I didn't even understand what was happening in this show, but the music was catchy—so catchy that we had to spend every night listening to those songs just to get her into the bathtub.

Then there was *Thomas and Friends*, *PAW Patrol*, *Doc McStuffins*, *WordGirl*, and *Daniel Tiger's Neighborhood*. Don't even get me started with *Wonder Pets!* I think I lost years of my life listening to that show.

However, if I'm being totally honest, there were some shows I secretly loved, like *Curious George*. But even though I loved it, George also drove me crazy. I mean, how many messes could one monkey make? And why was the Man with the Yellow Hat never around? Maybe he was the equivalent of a smoking mom—casual and clueless about where his child, or in this case monkey, was. I wanted to be as casual and clueless as the Man with the Yellow Hat, rarely bothered by George's endless curiosity.

Thinking back to that show, I wonder why I loved it so much. Maybe I loved it because even though the messes George made caused my blood pressure to rise, his curiosity piqued something in me. What a joy George's life seemed to be because of his curiosity! To me, he captured the essence of childhood wonder. What had happened to that wonder in me? What had happened to my own childhood curiosity? Why do adults grow up and out of curiosity?

Somewhere along the way, curiosity took a backseat to fear in my life. At some point, I learned that life is very uncertain. As a result, I felt like I needed to grab hold of certainty in order to feel at peace.

The older I got, the more measured I seemed to become. Whereas I'd once felt confident enough to be curious and try different jobs and move to different cities, I now was becoming more and more cautious. Whereas I once was driven by curiosity, now fear was speaking louder and louder.

Is the way I'm parenting going to completely ruin my kids?
Even though she's only six, will she always be a thief?
What if what I'm doing now affects her in a negative way in the future?
Why does her behavior cause me to feel so many emotions I never even knew existed?

See what I mean?

It's a wonder I haven't completely lost my mind. I don't think I've ever experienced a stage with my kids where parenting felt sure, certain, or without risk.

The older we get, the less curious we become in relationships, too. Deep down, I knew the only person I could control was myself. I resonate so much with what Elizabeth Gilbert says about creative living in her book *Big Magic*: "[Creative living is] about living a life that is driven strongly by curiosity [rather] than by fear."[1] Creative living in *all* of life. Not just in our professional life or our hobbies, but with people, too.

When we deal with people—with relationships—a level of vulnerability is always present. For me, this vulnerability was a reminder that relationships are never a sure thing. At any moment, someone could fall out of love or move on, and the relationship would end. The older I got, the more hurt I saw in relationships—and the more relationships I saw come to an end.

Curiosity is the opposite of certainty. Curiosity isn't about right or wrong or should or shouldn't. Those words are about certainty. And certainty is exactly how I approached life the older I got—especially with kids. I wanted certainty, no risk and no emotional exposure. I wanted someone to tell me what was right and what was wrong. I wanted to know what I should do and what I shouldn't do.

Would a C-section ruin my child for life?
Breastfeeding or bottle feeding?
Should babies eat, play, sleep or sleep, eat, play?
Do I spank or not?

What's the right school for my kids?
Will someone please give me the formula for parenting?

Fear was shouting at me from the backseat. I had forgotten how to be curious.

Curiosity made me nervous, because what if it led me the wrong way? What if I followed what I thought was the correct parenting formula and my girls didn't go to college because of it? You laugh, but I know you know exactly the kind of crazy I'm talking about. I'm obviously not finished parenting, but I can tell you that, so far, fear has not been my best guide.

Somewhere along the way, I started paying attention to how fear drove not just my parenting but my overall life. My daughters actually clued me in to this fact when they were little. How many times a day did the girls ask me, "Why?" Curiosity can be exhausting to those of us who feel comfort in certainty. Moreover, my girls' constant questioning revealed that I really disliked not having an answer. I also came to recognize that some of life's questions can't truly be answered. And that realization didn't sit well with me.

This is where I'm thankful for the personality pairing between my husband and me. He is naturally inquisitive, so where I would dismiss our daughters' questions, he welcomed them. He is a 5 on the Enneagram, which is described as the investigator. He loves learning and gathering information, whereas I feel like these actions would slow me down from achieving and crossing things off my to-do list. Many times the girls would ask their dad a question, unprepared for the wealth of information they were about to receive from him. But his inquisitive nature began to rub off on me. I started to remember how to be curious. I started to recall how to ask questions and wonder about things.

Here's what I've learned, though. If you incite your curiosity, prepare for people to be put off by it—especially if what you're raising questions about goes against what someone holds close to their heart.

When the girls were preschoolers, I had a pastor who sat down with me to inquire about this curiosity. Except he didn't view it as curiosity. He told me, "You and Scott question everything. How do you feel about raising your kids to be skeptics?" I was truly shocked. I had never viewed myself as a skeptic. I had started to see curiosity as something positive, but this pastor saw it as threatening, which is exactly how fear views curiosity. My response? I politely said that I welcomed their curiosity. I want my girls to grow up to be women who aren't afraid to ask questions. I don't want them to be women who blindly follow along. I want them to be women who wonder, women who figure out for themselves what is true instead of relying on someone to tell them. In my opinion, that makes for a stronger faith.

Sometimes fear wants to protect us—which I can appreciate. But it can also keep us stuck living a boring life. Elizabeth Gilbert says in *Big Magic*, "Your fear will always be triggered by your creativity, because creativity asks you to enter into the realms of uncertain outcome, and fear hates uncertain outcome."[2] Parenting and life are full of uncertain outcomes, but what if we miss the joy, curiosity, and wonder along the way because we allow fear to guide us?

Just because you follow your curiosity and experience something hard or painful doesn't mean you shouldn't have followed it. Scott and I could write a whole book on this idea. Back in 2010, we bought an old farmhouse in the historic district in the town where I grew up. Our curiosity was maxed out, and we designed and built the most beautiful house. But you know what happened? We spent more than we thought we would. We overextended ourselves in a not-so-great housing market. We ended up selling the house to move back to Atlanta and losing money. For many years, I viewed that farmhouse as a major regret. I wished we'd never attempted that renovation. But I've gradually shifted my view on it. We simply took a risk, and the risk didn't pan out. We jumped and experienced a crash landing. But here's what was good about that house. We both learned how much we enjoy design. We were able to flex our creative muscles. And we had fun and learned a lot in the process.

Curiosity may lead us to a dead end, but that doesn't mean it was wrong to explore. We weren't created to be flawless or to make perfect decisions. We live in an uncertain world—a world with hiccups. And we will miss out on so much of life if we refuse to allow curiosity to lead.

As the kids have gotten older, some of the early uncertainties have faded away, but new ones have appeared in their place. I no longer fear whether I nursed them long enough before introducing formula. But the new uncertainties feel greater, like more is at stake. And just like when they were little and fear would spike, I still reach for control.

One of the areas in parenting where fear fights curiosity the most is in regard to faith. I remember correcting six-year-old Sinclair for something she'd done wrong, but it felt all wobbly. It felt like I was trying to force a square peg into a round hole. As I explained to Sinclair that she needed to ask forgiveness from me for her wrong action, I also told her she needed to ask forgiveness from God. As someone who grew up evangelical, I had it drilled into me that no matter what "wrong" I've done, I must ask forgiveness from God. This logic never felt wonky to me until I looked into the face of my little girl. And even though it felt wonky, being the good Christian girl I was, I kept moving forward. Fear was yelling at me from the backseat, *If you don't get her to see her need for Jesus, she is screwed for eternity!*

That's when Scott stepped in, brave enough to interrupt me and say he didn't think we were going about this well. He stepped forward in the thick of vulnerability and uncertainty. At the risk of making me upset, he spoke up. And he was right. Sinclair could barely comprehend how her offense was wrong toward another person, let alone toward a God she couldn't see. So right then and there, we looked at fear and reminded it to sit quietly in the backseat. It's scary to do something different from how you were taught and how everyone around you is doing it. But we were curious. We wondered, *What difference would it make in our girls' lives if they didn't grow up fearing their actions, fearing that God was watching, feeling disappointed, and waiting for an apology?*

Curiosity is all about asking questions. And so I started asking questions about other parts of my faith. Curiosity allowed me to ask those questions freely. But most importantly, it allowed me to give my girls space to ask their own faith questions. Most likely because of my personality, I didn't grow up asking questions; I grew up just accepting what I was told. But I knew I wanted my girls to live curious lives instead of lives driven by fear, especially in regard to faith, and I knew I needed to model for them how to do this.

Scott and I had experienced enough as adults to know that life was far less clear and certain than we'd grown up believing. And after raising our girls for a while, we knew they both had a kid's natural ability to see life from different perspectives. We didn't want them to lose that.

So we made a choice about faith and our kids.

We thought about how to help them build a faith of their own. To do that, we wanted them to become women who can ask questions and think critically to determine what and why they believe something. When they were little, we said things like, "God loves you," and "God made you," but we avoided certain Bible stories that could lead to fear or cause confusion about God's love. Then, as they grew, we leaned into their natural curiosity—their developmental wiring to think like engineers and scientists. This may not be for everyone, but we stopped giving certain answers about faith to their curious questions. Instead, we replaced answers with questions like, "People believe a lot of different things. What do you think?" We want them to figure out for themselves what they believe so that they can develop a faith of their own—not just a neatly packaged faith that was handed to them.

We all know that there is nothing "neat" about life. Life is often messy and more gray than we imagined as children. We want our girls to hold space for the unknown. To ask questions. To be curious. To wonder. We tend to think that the opposite of faith is doubt, but the opposite of faith is certainty. Faith in its essence requires an ability to sit in the unknown—in what we cannot see. Raising my girls has highlighted the uncertainty of life. It has highlighted all the things I didn't know, all the things I couldn't understand, and all the things that didn't have a clear answer. But instead of decreasing my faith, it increased my faith—my ability to believe in what I cannot see and embrace the uncertainty instead of fearing it.

That's what I want for my girls. I don't want the unknown and uncertainty of life to bump up against what they always believed was certain to the point that it wrecks their faith. Instead, I want them to build their faith piece by piece through curiosity and questions.

One of the greatest gifts we can give our kids is an open-ended response. When we respond to their questions with curiosity instead of fear, our kids find freedom. They learn that curiosity is not the enemy. We have close friends who see it differently but still guide their kids toward curiosity. They still give certain answers and encourage them to ask questions. My point is that no matter how you choose to talk about faith with your kids, the goal is the same: for them to own their own faith. And curiosity is a wonderful guide.

When you are faced with questions from your kids about hard topics, your basic human instinct is to grab for certainty. But you can respond instead with your own curiosity. You have permission not to have all the answers. And when you ask your kids questions, you're teaching them to ask their own questions.

One day, our kids will hear other philosophies, other opinions, other interpretations, and we want them to have the tools to navigate the uncertain waters that rise around them. We don't want our kids to fall apart when life pokes a hole in their certainty. We want them to be able to sit in the uncertainty. When we respond with curiosity and questions instead of answers, we reenforce their ability to empathize. We give them the ability to leave room for other perspectives. These things allow for a bigger faith not a smaller one. Asking questions and thinking critically doesn't threaten the existence of our faith; instead, it has the potential to grow our faith. It helps establish a faith of our own.

Choosing to lean into our kids' curiosity feels uncertain,

uncomfortable, and sometimes scary. But isn't that how the world actually operates? We would all do well to sit in those moments and not fix uncertainty with a concrete answer when the world is full of people who see things in so many different ways.

The goal is not to create children who are "right." The goal is to create grown adults who can empathize, who can see the world from someone else's perspective and feel what they feel.

Not only did curiosity help me with my faith, but it also helped me get to know others and myself better. The more questions I began to ask about myself, the more I began to see myself more clearly. Who am I? What do I really want? What do I actually like? Those questions opened the door for me to discover more about my authentic self. Those questions started to burn in my soul the year before I turned forty. I longed to finally figure out who I am, but doing that took curiosity. It took asking questions and following where the answers led—and telling fear it was time to sit in the backseat.

Curiosity also helps me understand why I do what I do or why I feel what I feel. Until I had kids, I never paid attention to why I felt certain feelings. But when I had to start teaching my girls how to navigate their own feelings—both positive and negative—I quickly realized I needed to do the same.

Now when anger rises up in me, not only have I learned to (mostly) manage the emotions, but I've also learned to sit with myself after the fact to figure out why I felt that way. What triggered the anger in that moment? Why was that my response? The more I worked to figure out what was underneath, the calmer I became. Curiosity led me to peace.

Curiosity has also helped me learn to love others better. Without curiosity, I only saw myself. I saw my life and assumed everyone else lived similar lives. (Don't judge me too harshly for that.) But when I allowed curiosity to lead, I began to see others more clearly. As I asked questions about why someone might feel or act a certain way, I developed more perspective and empathy.

When Sinclair came home and told me about a girl kids were making fun of and calling gay, I asked questions. *Did the girl say this, or did others say this about her? How do you think she feels about this? How would you feel if you were that girl?* I watched as curiosity led my girl to empathy, perspective, and love.

Curiosity is what changed my views on LGBTQ. It helped me see more clearly why Black lives matter. It prompted me to imagine what it must be like to be a mother trying to cross the border with her children. Curiosity helps us believe the best about others because it leaves room for empathy and perspective.

A life driven by curiosity will lead to healing and peace. It will help you find ways to believe the best in yourself and others. It leads you to a truth that doesn't pit your faith against someone but instead stands for someone. Truth that helps you believe the best about yourself and others. Truth that doesn't pit your faith against someone but instead stands for someone.

Just look at the faces of the kids you are raising. Look at their expressions of wonder and curiosity as they walk through their world. As they grow older, fear will try to hijack their freedom, peace, and capacity to give and receive love. One of the greatest gifts we can give our children is to model a life led by curiosity.

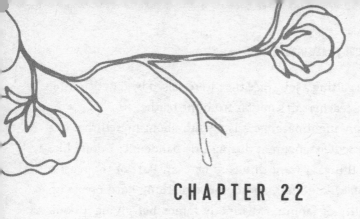

CHAPTER 22

YOU CAN DO HARD THINGS

My worst nightmare has happened.

Okay, before I tell you what happened, I will admit that I am being completely hyperbolic. I fully understand that worse things could have happened. But for the sake of exaggeration, hear me out.

So, my worst nightmare? A global pandemic hit in early 2020, and now the kids are home from school indefinitely and we can't leave the house. Now, I love my kids and I love my house, but my two kids equal at least four kids and my house is tiny. The challenge of finding time and space to work has reduced me to tears. Will I ever be alone again? (Cue all the tears.)

Not only am I supposed to write all the words of this book, but now I'm also in charge of my kids' education. I saw a meme the other day that implied that this generation of kids will have a hard time getting a job since they were raised by day-drinking homeschool teachers. It's not far from the truth.

Given my nightmare, here is a truth about myself that has been made acutely apparent during this pandemic: I don't like to do hard things. I want things to be easy. Part of the reason is that I don't like to fail, and doing something hard opens up the possibility of failure. I distinctly remember giving a book report in the third grade based on a book a preschooler could read. Heaven forbid I challenge myself. My personality also lends itself to wanting to move through things quickly for the sake of productivity and efficiency. The harder something is, the longer it takes to check off the list. And so I've always reasoned that if something is hard, I shouldn't do it. If I couldn't figure something out right away, it wasn't worth doing.

Now, keep in mind that I did a lot of things growing up. I was really great at piano and did well in almost any sport I tried. But if something seemed remotely difficult or required a little longer to figure out, I simply dismissed it. Moved on. Tried something else.

I think my avoidance of hard things involved something more than just my personality. As I grew up, I started to think it revealed some gaps in my theology—my thoughts about God and faith—too. So much of my faith fell into right and wrong categories. And somewhere along the way, I began to think that if something is hard, I must be doing it wrong. If something is hard, it must not be right. It appeared that life was pretty easy for most people in my church, especially in comparison to others around the world. Instead of seeing my easy life as privilege, I saw it as right versus wrong. Good versus bad. I would hear pastors and leaders explain that life is hard because of the fall of man. Sin entered the world, and that's why we have hard lives. Somehow, my wires got crossed, and I picked up a distorted view of the meaning of hard things (and I even have a seminary degree). Hard things looked like sin. I wanted to be void of sin, so naturally, I avoided hard things.

I wanted to be a good girl. I wanted to do everything right. And at some point I began to believe that whenever I faced a challenge, I must be doing the wrong thing. I allowed that understanding to determine what I was supposed to do, especially in regard to my professional life. If work was hard, I just needed to move on and find another job. Maybe I was supposed to be doing something else. (I changed jobs a lot in my career.)

This belief affected more than just my professional career. It affected my relationships, too. So imagine my surprise when I became a mother and found motherhood extremely difficult. *Maybe I shouldn't have done this*, I found myself thinking. *Maybe I shouldn't have become a mom.* The belief system I'd built caused me to view my child as a problem that needed fixing instead of a relationship to build. I was living my life—professionally and personally—with a fixed mindset. I believed difficult was just how motherhood was, and I had no ability to figure it out.

As a grown-up human, I've faced many hard things that have forced me to examine my theology and beliefs. Raising kids, dealing with my husband's illnesses and job losses, losing houses, losing friends. So many hard things over the years. My first reaction is always to blame myself. I must have done something wrong.

I could look at every hard thing listed above and try to come up with a reason for it. Maybe I drank too much coffee while pregnant. Maybe it was the C-section. Maybe it was a payback for something I did when I was younger. Maybe it was retribution for letting my high school boyfriend get to third base. Maybe it was a result of me wanting too much attention. In my mind, there *had* to be a reason—something I did wrong—for this hard thing to be happening.

But this theology—this way of seeing myself as the one to blame for every hard thing—started to crumble as my girls grew older. I began to realize that hard things happen because that's just how the world works. My girls weren't having a hard time in school because they drank too much cow's milk as toddlers. I started listening to myself talk to my girls when they faced hard things, and what came out of my mouth was far different from what I had told myself.

When Sinclair was seven, she was in a major Taylor Swift phase that even involved having bangs cut. She was committed. (And much like every woman in the world who has bangs cut, she immediately regretted it.) Naturally, she wanted to learn to play the guitar, so we signed her up for guitar lessons. She enjoyed the first lesson and wanted to continue to play at home. But this is where it all broke down. She couldn't figure it out. It just wasn't working quite like it did during her lesson, and soon she was on the floor in tears, crying about how terrible she was at guitar. She wanted to quit.

I asked her, "How long have you been playing the guitar?"

She responded with disgust, "Like, a day!"

I said, "More like an hour! Look at what you've learned in just an hour! You weren't born with the ability to pick up a guitar and automatically know how to play it. It doesn't work that way. It's hard, but you're gonna figure it out."

As I said those words, I thought of myself. How many times had I berated myself for not knowing how to do something the first time? How many times had I not attempted to do something out of fear of not doing it well the first time? How many times had I wanted to quit something because it was hard? It took seeing Sinclair writhing on the floor in angst for the truth to click in my head.

It's okay to not know how to do something. It's okay for something to be difficult. Just because a new endeavor is difficult doesn't mean you shouldn't do it. Just because it's difficult doesn't mean it's wrong. Just because it's difficult doesn't mean you've done something wrong.

As I'm raising my girls by this principle, I'm raising myself, too. I still want to avoid hard things. I see it in my girls, too. When I do, I have them repeat after me: *I can and I will.* And when I don't want to do the hard thing, I repeat the same words. *I can and I will.*

Some things are just going to require work. They are going to require effort. That doesn't make them wrong. It just makes them hard. *I can do hard things. I can and I will.*

Try to get published again? I can and I will.

Write a book in the middle of a pandemic? I can and I will.

Audition for a hosting job? I can and I will.

Move states . . . again? I can and I will.

So much good comes from doing hard things. The more you face hard things, the more resilience you build. Building resilience requires enduring some pain. Now, it's no secret that I don't like pain. I remember sitting in childbirth class with Scott while pregnant with Sinclair. As the nurse talked about the pain relief options, I looked at Scott and said, "I think I'll try to go as long as I can natural." He looked at me and sort of chuckled and said, "You don't even like to carry your own luggage. I'm not sure you're gonna like the pain of childbirth." Now, before you hate on him, you need to know that I laughed because he was 100 percent right. I don't like pain. I always look for an easier way for everything.

But even though I don't like pain, pain is what gets us to pay attention. We would skip right past so much of what we have learned in life if pain didn't prompt us to pay attention. I remember my chiropractor talking about this very thing—often the problem has been there for a while, but we don't notice it until we feel pain. When we avoid feeling the pain, we avoid healing, growing, and evolving. Yet we try so many ways to avoid pain, like controlling (hand raised), performing, perfecting, drinking, popping pills, shopping, or scrolling. The list goes on and on.

But what if pain exists to help us pay attention to what needs to happen? What if it is there to help us become more of what we were meant to be? What if it is there to remind us that we are human and we can do hard things?

Here's the problem: I like to evolve and grow, but do I really have to go through the hard and the painful? Can't I just read about it in a book? It doesn't work that way with pain. You don't dip your toe in the pool of pain and immediately understand it all. Often you have to do a cannonball into the deep end, then tread water for what feels like forever, in order to evolve.

I can look back with perspective and see how it was "good" that I felt such pain about my appearance—the hard evolved me. Heartbreak evolved me. Watching my husband lose it all evolved me. Seeing him sad and depressed and lost for two years evolved me. Raising girls has evolved me.

Pain brings growth and resilience. Pain teaches you that you can survive. And even though it hurts, resilience shows that *you can and you will.*

At the beginning of this chapter, I talked about my nightmare—writing this book in the middle of a global pandemic. I'm not going to lie. It has been hard. It hasn't been what I'd imagined. I imagined sending the girls off to school, then sitting with my coffee and laptop while creativity leapt from my brain onto the page. Instead, I had to write words while girls fought in the background. I had to work in a closet. I had to learn to write a few words here and a few words there. I had to learn to lean into the hard, the pain, because that's just part of life.

One of the greatest gifts we give ourselves and our kids is the opportunity to flex their "do hard things" muscle—to feel pain and build resiliency. Sinclair changed barns a couple of months ago. Riding at a new barn has brought new challenges. She has had to learn new vocabulary, new ways of controlling the horse, and new positions for jumping the horse. The learning curve has been steep. Today, she had a really hard lesson. She wanted to cry as she rode. She wanted to quit. But her trainer made her push through the hard to get to the other side.

As we drove home, Sinclair talked about how difficult the lesson had been. I responded, "I know. Hard things hurt sometimes. But I'm proud of you for pushing through. It shows that you can do hard things." This is her training ground. One day she will be a grown woman and face other hard things. My hope is that she will remember moments in the arena when she pushed through and didn't give up because it was hard. My hope is that she will remind herself she was made to do hard things.

I can and I will.

So how do you face hard things? Here's what I've done. When I'm in the middle of something hard, I acknowledge it's not easy. I say it out loud.

Writing a book in the middle of a pandemic is hard.

Homeschooling my kids while working full-time is hard.

Moving to another state is hard.

Not knowing how to parent is hard.

My husband losing his job is hard.

Being rejected is hard.

Then I give myself permission to feel what I feel. Somewhere along the way, we decided that feeling negative feelings wasn't okay. So we tried to pretend we were okay. We tried to act like we didn't actually feel sad, angry, or disappointed. However, nobody can dispute how you feel. Nobody can tell you it's not right to feel that way. Because it *is* okay to feel sad, discouraged, mad, tired. Part of accepting where you are—in the middle of the hard—is to allow yourself to feel what you feel. You also need to speak out those feelings. I usually speak them out in my journal first. I process what is happening and what I'm feeling. But finding a trusted friend you can speak out loud to can be helpful as well.

The hard doesn't automatically go away because you acknowledge it. It's a matter of leaning in and doing the work. My favorite episode to record every year is the end-of-year recap with my friend Merica, where we talk about what we've learned that year. At the end of 2018, I told her I learned that even though it would be hard, I just needed to do the work. I had circled around some different ideas for several years, but the hardship of it—the pain of it—had caused me to avoid taking action. But no more. It was time to do the work. (And this book you are reading is the product of doing the work.)

When life is hard, acknowledge the hard. Feel what you feel. Speak it out. Do the work.

In the middle of hard things, we often use the word *hope*. This word is used in relation to both serious and lighthearted needs.

I hope I get that parking spot.

I hope that guy will ask me out.

I hope we get the house.

I hope I don't lose my job.

For many years, hope felt like a lofty thing I had no control over, like I was just hoping God would look my way and act on my behalf. Hope also felt like something I could easily get wrong— like placing my hope in the wrong thing, place, or person. That very word could even make me feel guilty. When Scott and I went through a hard season after his business failed, I felt like hope was choking me. I remember someone saying, "Well, that's because you put your hope in the wrong thing. You didn't put your hope in God." But that wasn't necessarily true.

The more I've studied hope, the more I understand that hope isn't a feeling. Hope isn't determined by or built upon someone else. Hope is a way of thinking. Hope is about resourcefulness and resiliency. It's about figuring out what you want to do and where you want to go, knowing that you are capable. Hope is the ability to set realistic goals, figure out how to reach those goals, and believe that you *can* reach them.

When I faced the goal of writing this book in the middle of the pandemic, I applied this hopeful self-talk. The following is taken from my journal in mid-March 2020, when the girls came home from school:

The goal is to write the book by August 1.

The plan? Write 2,500 words a week. Write on Tuesdays, Thursdays, and Fridays. Work from Scott's closet those days.

And even though it will be hard, believe in yourself that you can do it. Keep showing up. You can figure this out.

I can do hard things. I can and I will.

I can and I will is hopeful self-talk. It doesn't look like wishing upon a star. It doesn't look like waiting on someone else to solve your problem or remove you from the difficult circumstance. While I sometimes feel like I would love to be rescued, hope doesn't do that. Hope knows where you want to go, gives you the grit to work hard, and then keeps you believing that you can do it—you can do hard things. You were created to do hard things. That is as true as the sun rising. If you've ever given birth, run a marathon, or endured any amount of time playing pretend play with your kids then you know that you can do hard things.

Whatever you are facing, you can do hard things. Raising a difficult child? Facing the end of a marriage? Looking sickness in the eye? Finding a new job? You are capable. As my friend Sissy Goff says to girls who are overcome with anxiety, "You are braver, stronger, and smarter than you think you are." You can do hard things. *You can and you will.*

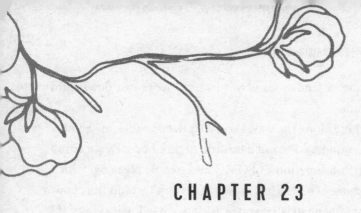

CHAPTER 23

SAY YES

One thing I've realized when it comes to raising kids—especially kids with a certain fight to them—is that they hear *no* a lot. I mean, if I conducted a research project on how many times I say the word *no*, I bet the number would be shocking. But in my defense, usually the *no* comes for good reason.

No, you can't touch the hot stove.

No, you can't have candy for breakfast.

No, you can't stay up until midnight.

No, no, no.

Sometimes we need to say no to protect our kids from hurting themselves or others. But as with any demanding job or relationship, at some point, we get tired. And our *no* starts to show up outside of the realm of safety.

Can you play with me right now? *No.*

Can you help me? *No.*

Can I rearrange my room? For the hundredth time, *no.*

The requests tend to bombard us until we're just downright tired and done.

Somewhere along the way, I was surprised to realize just how often I was saying *no*. I'm not a *no* kind of girl. I usually succumb to the lethal combination of FOMO and people pleasing, which means I'm more of a *yes* kind of girl. If I think I would hurt your feelings by saying *no* to what you're asking of me, I will say *yes*. If I think I'll miss out on whatever event you are inviting me to (even though deep down I might not want to go), I'll say *yes*. Usually my go-to response is *yes*, but not with my kids. I started noticing that *no* was becoming my default response to them, which made me reconsider whether I wanted to be a *no* kind of girl or a *yes* kind of girl.

What if I decided to say *yes* sometimes?

Isn't it interesting how much power that little word holds? I bet you love to hear *yes* from people. *Yes* may be our favorite word when we're on the receiving end of it.

Can we grab coffee? *Yes!*

Can we go to the Braves game? *Yes!*

Can we sleep in on Sunday? *Yes!*

Here's something I've learned: Saying *yes* highlights why I said *no* to so many things. When I looked at the *no*s, I could see a few common reasons rise up: fear, control, selfishness, sheer exhaustion. These reasons have been especially true in motherhood. If I say *yes*, what if my girls get hurt? What if they destroy something? I realized I wanted control of the situation. For instance, I was the kind of mom who was always thinking ahead about how to have an easy bedtime experience. So I controlled everything I could to make sure we were working toward that goal. But mostly, I said *no* to things I just didn't want to do so we could arrive at bedtime that much faster.

As much as we love hearing *yes*, it's not always easy to be the one giving that answer—especially to people who drain us. (I'm looking at you, dear children.)

It's hard to say *yes* when your kids have pushed every single button you have (including buttons you didn't even know existed).

It's hard to say *yes* when you haven't slept through the night since who knows when.

It's hard to say *yes* when your children have literally wrecked almost everything you own.

But what if you decided to say *yes* anyway?

I've found that saying yes to my kids has done so much to enrich our relationship with each other. It has sealed the cracks where I felt disconnected. That's because yes can change a relationship. Try it out for yourself. When your partner asks for something, respond with yes when you normally would say no, and see what happens. When your friend who always asks to get together—but you put it off because you always think you're too busy—asks again, say yes, and see what happens.

Yes can change a relationship.

One relationship that I wanted to change was with my kids, so I decided to start saying yes more. I began asking myself if saying no was necessary. I'd check myself in those moments right before I said no and ask myself if it was possible to say yes instead.

Yes to playing LEGOs.

Yes to building the fort.

Yes to letting her play with every single toy she owns, even if she makes a mess.

Yes to letting her help cook dinner.

Yes to spontaneous dance parties.

Yes to crafting, even though a mess will likely follow. (But let the record note that I will *always* say *no* to glitter and slime. There are absolutes in this house.)

I also asked myself why I wanted to say no. Usually it was because I just didn't want to do it. I find playing LEGOs or Barbie or American Girls horrifically boring. I also hate messes, so if I anticipate that the activity will create a mess, I almost automatically say no. But what's the harm in pretend play? What's the harm in painting that pumpkin? The last time I checked, a relationship is more than just me. Saying no revealed that I saw my girls as interfering with my life.

Sometimes I say no because I'm frustrated with them or stressed about something. Pro tip: I've found that the art of distraction works the same on parents as it does on babies. If a baby is upset, often they can be distracted by something else. Likewise, if you find yourself frustrated, create a distraction. Head to Starbucks where everyone gets a treat. Or go to the park where everyone can run out that frustration. Say yes to something different.

A powerful bond is built between parent and child every time we say yes. I'm not saying you have to say yes to everything, but I'm saying to pay attention. Open yourself up to consider saying yes more. If you hear yourself saying no to everything, choose to say yes the next time. My friend Joni Lay of the blog *Lay Baby Lay* has a standing "yes day" with her girls. On that particular day, she says yes to everything. You want a lunch of Cheetos, candy corn, and ice cream? Yes. She talks about how much her girls look forward to that day and how it actually *is* so much fun.

Saying yes has the power to shift your perspective and posture toward your child. I notice that when I say yes, the climate around me seems different. My mood is better. I think I smile more. We all smile more. I fully believe that our children long for us to delight in them. In fact, I know it's true because that's how I felt as a child. *Yes* is the ultimate verbal confirmation of delight. It tells your kids that you want to build a connection with them.

My girls would light up as I said yes . . .

to being goofy
to doing something spontaneous
to getting ice cream because it's Tuesday

Saying yes has helped build my children up. Saying yes has allowed them to be who they are, not who I am. In my home, everything has a place. A messy room makes me feel like I can't think. My creative daughter has a place for things, but her way of organizing differs from mine. What looks messy to me makes perfect sense to her. I had to make sure her room was uncluttered enough to move through in case of emergency, but outside of that, I needed to allow her to arrange her room in her own way. I needed to say yes to her needs.

Every time we say yes, we are injecting positive energy into our relationships. That little word *yes* has the power to change our parenting.

Saying yes is something we have to practice. It's not just about changing our attitude. It's a genuine practice. Eventually this practice of saying yes to my kids started to change the way I saw myself in the world. I realized that at some point in motherhood my posture of *no* began applying not just to my kids but also to opportunity. Saying no felt safer. What if I fail? What if I'm not the best? What if I look foolish? No had become a self-protection mechanism for me.

I ignored what I really wanted to say, think, do, or experience and I said no. No to writing. No to playing tennis. No to learning the guitar. No to dancing at that wedding. No. But deep down, I wanted to do those things.

Something about turning forty really exposed the armor I wore. I realized I wanted more out of life. And to get more, you can guess which word needed to be replaced. So I started saying *yes* instead of *no*.

Yes to writing—even if it meant facing rejection.

Yes to playing tennis—even if it meant I wouldn't be any good at it.

Yes to dancing with Rory at a wedding—even if I looked silly doing it.

And just like my relationship with my girls changed after I started saying *yes*, my relationship with myself began to change. I began to feel more like me. I began to feel freer. I worried less about failure. In fact, I even welcomed it. I started to look for things to do that might result in failure because I wanted to show myself I would survive even if I failed. I wanted to prove to myself that failing wouldn't be the end of me.

The older we get and the more responsibilities we carry, the greater our tendency to self-protect becomes. We fear, we control, we worry. And we say *no*. But what would it look like to say *yes* more? How would saying *yes* improve your relationships? How would saying *yes* improve yourself? How would saying *yes* help you try new things and have more fun in life?

For most of us, saying *yes* isn't our gut reaction, which means we need to retrain ourselves to say yes. When "No" is about to leave your lips, just pause and ask yourself why you're about to say no. Check the armor. And reconsider your response.

This single practice of saying yes has the power to completely change your relationships . . . with your children, your partner, your friends, your coworkers, your family, your neighbors. By saying yes to my kids, I slowly started to see how that little word was changing the dynamic between us. But it was also changing me. I found myself feeling more confident and enjoying life more. Saying yes truly has the power to shift not only your relationships but also the way you see yourself in the world.

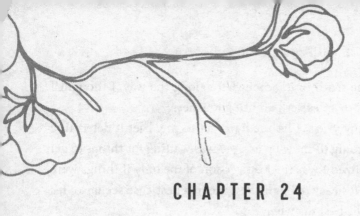

CHAPTER 24

SHOW UP AS YOUR BEST SELF

Sometimes I wonder if I tallied up all the hard parenting days, would they outnumber the easy ones? I knew there would be difficult things like lack of sleep during the newborn stage, but I was not prepared for the emotional warfare inherent in parenting. In fact, wrong expectations did me a disservice for a long time. I would often hear myself saying, "It's not supposed to be this hard." Maybe it was my natural bent toward optimism, but I had always assumed that parenting was supposed to be joyful and pleasant.

That assumption reveals a flaw in my belief system. I equated joyful with easy. If something is easy, then it's joyful. Never did I equate joy with pain or difficulty. I recently heard someone say, "Anytime you're thinking it's not working or shouldn't be this hard, your end result is entitlement." Wow. That sort of hurts.

But I see the truth in it. Somewhere along the way, I thought I was entitled to an easier parenting journey.

For many years, I let the hard get to me. I let it determine who I was going to show up as. As I was waiting for things to get easier, I realized I was the best version of me only if things were going well. It's easy to be the best me in a best-case scenario. It's easy to be the best me when . . .

I'm not running late.
My kids obey the first time.
My husband is happy in his job.
I enjoy cooking.
My kids aren't fighting.
I know how to help my daughters.

When the stars align and the sun shines, I show up as the best version of myself. But when things go awry, a different me shows up. It's hard to be my best when . . .

Traffic keeps me from picking up my kid from school
    on time.
I have to repeat myself 8 billion times to pick the towel up
    off the floor.
My kids have made yet another mess without cleaning up
    the other messes.
I'm trying to work from home and I'm constantly
    interrupted.
I've burned dinner . . . again.
My kids wake up fighting, go to bed fighting, and eat, sleep,
    and breathe fighting.

My daughter yells at me and says hurtful things.

When any of those things happen, I don't show up as the best version of myself—at all. How am I supposed to show up as my best self when life is hard?

Before I could answer that question, I had to figure out what my best self actually looks like. Raising kids has taught me what my worst self looks like simply because parenting has been the hardest thing I've ever done. My worst self is angry, resentful, hurtful, dismissive, sarcastic, and cold. Not a pretty list. But in those moments when life is hard and I choose to show up as my best self, I am . . .

Calm
Curious
Empathic
Connected
Relaxed
Unhurried

What a difference!

I remember one particular fight I had with Sinclair when she was in sixth grade. If you've ever raised a tween, you know their armor and mode of defense. Middle school girls know how to fight. (I sometimes wonder if middle school is actually just a military training facility.)

Often during fights with my daughter, I felt like I'd brought a knife to a gunfight. (Thanks, Taylor, for that simile.) I remember one particular fight that happened at the end of the day. (They usually do. After we've both experienced a full day of All. The.

193

Things.) I couldn't tell you what we fought over, but it escalated quickly to yelling. I'm pretty sure it was like a poker game: "I see your crazy and I raise you off-the-charts crazy." Sometimes it's like I've come out of my body and am watching what happens from above. The whole time, I'm thinking, *Sarah, you're acting crazy! You need to stop this train.* But it's like I'm just a spectator at the show who can't get off the crazy train.

After it was all said and done, we went to our separate corners. I spent some time coming back to my rational, thinking brain, and when I did, I approached my daughter. I said, "I don't think either one of us showed up as our best selves today. And I'm sorry. I want you to know that I will try to show up as my best self next time." We described what our best selves would look like in a disagreement and agreed to try to show up as them next time.

Showing up as our best selves takes practice and perseverance and a whole lot of grace. For a recovering perfectionist, that's hard. It goes back to what I said earlier. When I have the false expectation that life isn't supposed to be this hard, I set myself up for failure. I have to do the work of figuring out who my best self is and then maintain that self when faced with difficulty.

Imagine what could happen if our best selves showed up when we were angry, frustrated, or hurt.

I love baseball, specifically the Atlanta Braves. I've loved them my whole life, and now we live only about fifteen minutes from the stadium. We are season ticket holders, and it's our favorite date night and family experience. We know all the players and cry when they are traded. They're like family to us. (Stalker status alert.) Here's the deal about baseball: The season is extremely long. Teams play 162 games in the regular season. And while the regular season is long, the off-season is short. Most players have three to four months off before reporting back to their team for spring training. And what a player does during the off-season is very important in determining how well they will play during the regular season. What you do in the off-season determines how well you will do in-season.

The same is true with parenting, and life in general, when it comes to showing up as our best selves. You can't expect to show up as your best self in the heat of the moment without working on becoming your best self in the off-season.

What helps you become your best self?

For me, sleep is a big part of the equation. I show up as an angry grizzly bear when I don't get enough sleep. That's part of the reason parenting newborns and littles was so very hard for me. With newborns, sleep is the first thing to go. I try to get around seven hours of sleep each night. And if I find myself overly tired during the day, I give myself permission to take a quick power nap or at least to rest.

I also need time to myself in order to be my best self. When I don't get enough breathing space, I hop on the crazy train real fast. Maybe that's because I'm part introvert and need just a little bit of alone time in order to recharge. As a mom, you are rarely alone when raising kids. For heaven's sake, you can't even go to the bathroom alone when your kids are little. Because I know I need regular time-outs, I do what I can to make time and space for myself—even in the middle of a pandemic. Let's just say I've been taking a lot of smoke breaks (aka walks).

Journaling is also helpful for me. Journaling helps me process all that I'm feeling. It's a place for me to get it all out. I have laid out some dark things on the pages of those Moleskine journals. I often tell my daughters to write it out. Say all the things you want to say in that journal. Getting it out of your head and onto the paper can be a powerful thing.

I also do my best to practice gratitude. A daily practice of gratitude has really helped me. Putting effort into seeing the good in ordinary things helps me to have a sense of calm and act like my best self.

Meditation is a new practice to me. I've learned in recent years that I'm more of a breath holder than a deep breather. In an effort to help my girls manage their own emotions, I've learned some good stuff about meditation. Science proves that when we are operating with our engines on high, our brains can't actually think. That's why it's important to take time to breathe when you're worked up. Meditation is an opportunity to practice breathing in the off-season.

One thing I value almost more than anything is connecting with friends. When I'm not connecting in a real way with others, I find my worst self coming out. That's why I make sure to schedule at least one engagement a week with a friend. When time with friends is a part of my life, I'm more likely to operate as my best self.

The list could go on and on.

Opportunities to do things I love.

Time away from the kids.

Reading.

Most of the examples above are things I do to take care of myself in the off-season so that when tension rises, my best self can rise to the top. But I've also noticed a perspective shift in me that happens when I'm my best self. I've learned how important it is to have realistic expectations of other people and a generous response toward them when those expectations go unmet. Being in relationship with people isn't easy. When someone is being difficult with me, my worst self assumes the worst about them, but my best self maintains a more generous view. I didn't fully understand this dynamic until something happened at the farm where Sinclair rides horses.

Being at the farm makes me feel like we're a thousand miles away from home. We can hear all the sounds around us and see the stars light up the sky at night. One particular Monday, a new horse, Vegas, was being ridden during Sinclair's lesson. Vegas had come from a farm where she'd experienced some neglect. Because Vegas wasn't used to being around other horses, she was having a hard time riding in a lesson alongside other horses.

Something happened and Vegas spooked, throwing her rider off. There were about five girls on horses in the arena at the moment. Everyone came to a stop as Vegas bolted around the arena, looking to escape. I watched as Sinclair froze on her own horse, holding still. I knew she was likely very afraid of what was happening around her, but I watched her keep her horse calm as Vegas ran circles around her. The trainer finally got hold of Vegas and led her back to her stall.

When Sinclair's lesson was over and I was waiting for her to turn her horse out to pasture, I walked up to Vegas in the stall. Her eyes took me in as I rubbed her nose and said, "It's OK. I know it's scary, but you're gonna figure it out." It dawned on me in that moment that this is what my best self looks like. Instead of being frustrated with the horse, I had a generous response toward her.

Isn't that what we all want to hear, especially in those moments when we feel afraid or incapable? In moments when we show up as our worst self? *It's okay. I know it's scary, but you're gonna figure it out.* It dawned on me later that sometimes my children are just like Vegas—scared horses trying to figure it out. What if I approached them with the same kindness and empathy? What if instead of anger, I chose compassion and understanding?

When she throws game pieces across the table.

When she rolls her eyes.

When she spews back hurtful words.

When tears flood her eyes.

Maybe she's just a scared horse. Maybe she just needs someone to look her in the eye and say, "It's okay. I know you're afraid or worried or hurt, but you're gonna figure it out."

Who is like the scared horse in your life? Maybe it's your child or your partner. Maybe it's your parent or friend. Or maybe it's you. Showing up as your best self starts with generosity in your thoughts toward yourself and others. And then think about what it would look like if you took care of yourself in the off-season before the hard happens. You have it in you to determine who you are going to show up as. Imagine what your relationships would look like if, when life squeezed hard, you showed up as your best self.

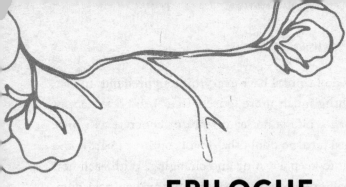

EPILOGUE

Raising kids has taught me . . . well, me.

I've had to come face-to-face with who I thought I was supposed to be and who I actually am and who I want to become. I've seen my privilege. I've seen my selfishness. I've seen all sorts of things that have needed improvement.

It would be easy for me to look back with regret, wishing I hadn't had to learn the hard way about so many things. It would be easy to judge my past self and wonder why I didn't see then what I see now. It would be easy to be mad at myself, but that's just part of growing up. Part of becoming.

Yes, raising kids has been hard, but it has pushed me to become more *me*. And that is the greatest gift I've ever received. When people would say that children are a gift from God, I would deep down reject that belief. I'd give a fake smile and barely agree. Kids never felt like a gift to me because most of the gifts I received in my life weren't difficult. But when I view my girls in this light, as the catalyst for change in me, then yes, they are absolute gifts. I am forever grateful for the ways that raising them has in turn raised me.

In no way do I think I have everything figured out. In fact, I hold everything much more loosely than I did five, ten, or twenty years ago. Life is not as certain or concrete as I once thought it was. I have no doubt that I will continue to grow and change. I *want* to keep learning and changing. With each new year, each new hardship, each new opportunity, I gain wisdom. I heard Goldie Hawn say on Oprah's *Master Class* podcast, "The beauty of getting older is the surprise of what else you can do to make the world a better place with the wisdom you've accrued over those years."[1] I hope this book helps the world become a better place.

At the end of the day, I want to be someone who feels free to reconsider things about life, myself, faith, and this world for years to come. Yes, that can feel uncertain, but it can also leave room for a lot of imagination—a lot of wonder.

Raising myself is the best thing I can do for my girls, because when I accept who I really am, when I start to live out who I really am, when I start to trust who I really am, that's when I am free.

What we are doing matters. Doing the hard work of integrating our lives—making what is on the outside match what is on the inside—is important because our kids are watching. We are modeling for them what it looks like to be humans who are becoming, evolving, and growing. We are modeling what it looks like to do the work of discovering who you are and then living it out loud.

As I step into the freedom of being fully me, I want to give my girls permission to discover who they really are. I want to give them permission to bump into life, faith, relationships, and the world. I want to give them permission to fail. The more freedom I find for myself, the more accepting I become. The more loving I become. The more generous I become. What a gift to give this freedom not only to myself, but also to my girls.

So many of the great freedom fighters have fought because the real freedom is found in setting others free.

I set myself free so that you will be free.

I set myself free so that my girls will be free.

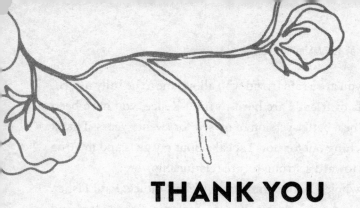

THANK YOU

To my readers. Thank you for picking up this book and spending some time with me. I truly want to be your cheerleader and your guide, to help you survive your life right where you are.

To the women who have raised me. I've experienced so many providential relationships over the course of my life. Relationships that, for a season, have helped shape and grow me. They have helped me become a better version of myself.

To my friends who have called, texted, emailed, sent DMs, and shown up to celebrate me throughout this whole process. Connection is one of my top values, and having you on my team brings me such delight. You have encouraged me, challenged me, and spoken life into me.

To Lesley Graham, for our weekly "smoke breaks." Walking with you each week through this process helped me to navigate my thoughts and feelings. I will forever be grateful for those moments of sanity.

To Sarah Anderson and Kellee Hall. Thank you for painstakingly reading all the words of this book before it ever reached an editing phase. Your opinions and perspectives mean the world to me. Sarah, you are a safe friend who allows me to be fully myself. Those kinds of friends are hard to find. Kellee, you have been helping me be a better version of myself for twenty years. Thank you for watching out for how I speak about my girls and making sure I work toward a strong future relationship.

To the whole Zondervan team—Webb Younce, Paul Fisher, Harmony Harkema, Alicia Kasen, Stefanie Schroeder, and Andrea Kelly. Thank you for believing in me and being excited for this book from the very beginning. Working with a team is so much fun because every time someone speaks into or touches the project, it only gets better. You have made me better.

To Carolyn McCready. I felt like I hit the jackpot when you said you would be my editor. You have such an ease about you that puts me at peace whenever we speak. And your ever-accepting ways always make me feel welcome at the table.

To my literary agent, Mike Salisbury. Every phone call, email, and voice memo (even though you hate those) has been helpful, encouraging, and fun. Thank you for believing in me and being my champion through this process. I remember telling Scott after our first conversation that I felt free to show up exactly as I am with you. Thank you for taking a chance on me.

To my mom and dad. So much of who I am has your fingerprints all over it. You taught me to laugh, to love, to dream, and to work hard. Thank you for pouring your lives into me, not only to give me a better life, but to give me the courage to chase my dreams. Success as a parent isn't in how well our kids turn out but in how much those kids want to come home. And given the fact that our family moved back to live next door to you says a lot about your success as parents.

To my girls, Sinclair and Rory. Thank you for raising me.

You are the single greatest motivation for growth and change for the better in me. I know I'm not doing it all right, but I hope you will build upon the foundation we are creating and that you fly higher, love more freely, and enjoy life more fully. I want you to be curious, trust yourselves, and be brave with your lives. You are loved no matter what you do, say, or think.

To Scott. Thank you for going first. You listened to the truth inside you. You spoke up. You were curious and questioned. Our marriage and relationships with our girls are better because of that. You allowed me to discover who I really am and to experience being loved no matter what. You were the one who insisted that we speak words of love and acceptance over our girls every day. You were the one who insisted that certain fears for our girls needed to be swept off the table. You were the one who modeled curiosity. You were the one who led the way. So for all of that, thank you.

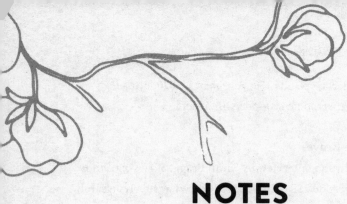

NOTES

Introduction

  1. Rachel Macy Stafford, *Live Love Now* (Grand Rapids: Zondervan, 2020), 15.

Chapter 1: Tell the Truth

  1. David Kessler, "David Kessler and Brené on Grief and Finding Meaning," interview by Brené Brown, *Unlocking Us* podcast, March 31, 2020, https://brenebrown.com/podcast /david-kessler-and-brene-on-grief-and-finding-meaning/.

Chapter 4: You Belong Here

  1. Brené Brown, *The Gifts of Imperfection* (Center City, MN: Hazelden Publishing, 2010), 25.

Chapter 5: What Made You Smile Today?

  1. Brené Brown, *The Gifts of Imperfection* (Center City, MN: Hazelden Publishing, 2010), 78.

  2. Will Arnett, interview by Dax Shepard, *Armchair*

Expert podcast, episode 178, February 3, 2020, https://armchairexpertpod.com/pods/will-arnett.

Chapter 6: Be Brave

1. Sarah Anderson, interview by Sarah Bragg, *Surviving Sarah* podcast, episode 2, December 22, 2015, www.survivingsarah.com/blog/episode-2-sarah-anderson.

Chapter 9: I Could Be Wrong

1. Susan Clarke and CrisMarie Campbell, interview by Sarah Bragg, *Surviving Sarah* podcast, episode 213, December 22, 2015, www.sarahbragg.com/survivingsarah/213.

2. Brené Brown, *Rising Strong* (New York: Spiegel & Grau, 2015), 77–97.

Chapter 11: Take a Smoke Break

1. Sissy Goff, David Thomas, and Melissa Trevathan, *Are My Kids on Track? The 12 Emotional, Social, and Spiritual Milestones Your Child Needs to Reach* (Minneapolis: Bethany House, 2017), 44.

Chapter 15: You Can Trust Her—Your Body

1. "Over Half of U.S. Teens Have Had Sexual Intercourse by Age 18, New Report Shows," Centers for Disease Control and Prevention, June 22, 2017, https://www.cdc.gov/nchs/pressroom/nchs_press_releases/2017/201706_NSFG.htm.

Chapter 19: Me Too

1. Brené Brown, *I Thought It Was Just Me* (New York: Avery, 2008), 38.

Chapter 21: Be Curious

1. Elizabeth Gilbert, *Big Magic* (New York: Riverhead Books, 2015), 9.

2. Elizabeth Gilbert, *Big Magic* (New York: Riverhead Books, 2015), 23.

Epilogue

1. "Goldie Hawn," *Oprah's Master Class* podcast, May 2, 2019, https://omny.fm/shows/oprah-s-master-class-the-podcast /goldie-hawn#description.